EXPLOR
ELIZABETH LINE

Jeff Lock

COUNTRYSIDE BOOKS
NEWBURY BERKSHIRE

First Published 2022
Countryside Books, Newbury, Berkshire
© 2022 Jeff Lock
Updated and reprinted 2023

Acknowledgements

The publication of this book could not have been achieved without the help of my walking friends and family: Alan, Alison, Ann, Claire, Dave, Duncan, Eddie, Gillian, Günter, Helen, Jan, Jim H., Jim W., Linda, Mike and Sonia. Between them, they have suggested routes, tested the walks and given feedback on the walk descriptions. Particular thanks to my wife Gillian for acting as critic and editor. I am also indebted to the Crossrail press releases, which have provided a wealth of information on the Elizabeth line, and to Wikipedia and the many local and national organisations whose websites have contributed to the additional background information shown for many of the walks. Special thanks also to Alex Batho at Countryside Books for her support and encouragement.

Disclaimer

The walk descriptions are believed to be correct at the time of printing. However, things do not always stay the same and the author does not accept responsibility for any subsequent variations. While the walks are suitable for anyone with a reasonable level of fitness, liability cannot be accepted for any personal loss or injury which might occur when using this guide.

Maps

The map for each walk is based on information from OpenStreetMap®. OpenStreetMap® is open data, licensed under the Open Data Commons Open Database License (ODbL) by the OpenStreetMap Foundation (OSMF). OpenStreetMap® and its contributors are hereby credited.

Photos

All the photos were taken by the author with the exception of the images on page 6, which are reproduced courtesy of Herrenknecht AG, manufacturer of the Crossrail tunnel boring machines.

ISBN 978 1 84674 414 3

All materials used in the manufacture of this book carry FSC certification.

Produced by Letterworks Ltd., Reading
Printed by Holywell Press, Oxford

Contents

Elizabeth Line

London's Newest Railway
Delivered by Crossrail

Explore London's Newest Railway

This book celebrates the opening of the Elizabeth line - London's newest railway. The line is a major feat of engineering that delivers improved connectivity and shorter journey times across London and the South East and opens up opportunities for new walks and excursions. For everyone, there is the chance to visit new places and see new sights. This book contains 23 walks designed to foster a spirit of exploration along the east-west trajectory of the Elizabeth line. Each walk starts at a Crossrail station and many are designed to create new routes between communities linked by the Elizabeth line.

- 12 start at one Crossrail station and finish at another.
- 6 are circular and finish at the same station.
- 5 finish at a different station on the underground or mainline railway network.

As an added bonus, if you have a Freedom Pass issued by a London Borough you can currently travel the whole of the Elizabeth line free of charge.

Communities East and West Connected by Crossrail

The Elizabeth line connects Shenfield in the east to Reading in the west. The line consists of two existing, but improved, railway lines from Liverpool Street to Shenfield and from Paddington to Reading, with a new underground section beneath Central London. There is also a south-eastern spur to Abbey Wood and a western link to Heathrow.

A direct rail route across London from east to west had been a vision for over 35 years, but it was not until 2001 that Crossrail Limited was established as a wholly owned subsidiary of Transport for London to deliver that vision. In 2008, an Act of Parliament confirmed the route of the new line and Crossrail finally broke ground on 15 May 2009 at Canary Wharf, when the first pile was driven into the North Dock at the site of the new Canary Wharf Station. Initially simply referred to as 'Crossrail', the new railway was named in honour of Queen Elizabeth II, who officially opened the line on 17 May 2022. Operated by Transport for London (TfL), passenger services on the Elizabeth line started on 24 May 2022.

Crossrail in Numbers
- 113 km of track
- 42 km of new tunnels beneath the heart of London
- 3 million cubic metres of concrete used
- 10 new stations
- 31 improved stations
- 70 new trains
- £18.9 billion cost
- 200 million passenger journeys expected annually
- 1.5 million more people brought within 45 minutes of Central London

New Stations
The sheer size of the new underground spaces created by Crossrail has led to comparisons with cathedrals. Indeed, at around 250m, most of the platforms are 100m longer than St Paul's Cathedral. The innovative use of sprayed concrete in the tunnels allows for smooth bends, which improve the passenger flow. Aesthetically, it also creates a harmonious feel. The overall impression created is one of space and clarity and the use of natural light wherever possible adds to the sense of awe.

The 10 new stations are Abbey Wood, Bond Street, Canary Wharf, Custom House, Farringdon, Liverpool Street, Paddington, Tottenham Court Road, Whitechapel and Woolwich. While they share a common design at platform level, each ticket hall and exterior has its own distinct character, often reflecting the heritage of the local area.

At Whitechapel a walkway connects the areas north and south of the railway and a bell-ringing pattern is featured in the cladding to pay homage to Whitechapel Bell Foundry.

At Crossrail Place the roof garden displays plants from across the world and a new bridge connects the two very different communities of Poplar and Canary Wharf.

At Woolwich the columns show the regimental colours of the artillery companies based at the Royal Arsenal and the entrance shows an expanded design of the WWI 'dead man's penny'.

At Farringdon the heavy metal gates are based on a barcode for the word 'Farringdon' and the ticket hall design references the nearby jewellery quarter.

At Liverpool Street the grooved ceilings reflect the pinstripes of the traditional city workers' suits.

At Tottenham Court Road the western exit with its dark, cinematic colours celebrates the night economy of Soho. The eastern exit features a work by Turner Prize artist Richard Wright.

The other 31 stations on the network have been upgraded to provide a better passenger experience, including brighter and more spacious ticket halls, improved accessibility and step-free access to platform level, new lifts and footbridges, clearer signage, help points, information screens and CCTV and staff available until the last train.

Natural Light at Woolwich

Crossrail Tunnelling

© Herrenknecht AG

For more than three years, eight tunnel boring machines (TBMs), built in Germany, were hard at work 150m beneath the streets of central London, to create 42 kilometres of new tunnels. Each 1,000-tonne machine had an external diameter of 7.1m and was 150m in length. Operated by gangs of 20 engineers working in shifts around the clock, the average rate of progress was 38 metres a day. The concrete used to create the tunnel linings is designed to last for at least 120 years.

As a sign of good luck and in honour of Saint Barbara, the patron saint of miners, 38 statues of St Barbara were blessed and placed at each of the entrances and other strategic points in the tunnels and remained in place till the tunnelling was complete. It is also a tradition that a tunnel boring machine should not start work until it has been given a woman's name. The Crossrail TBMs, which work in pairs, were named by schoolchildren, as well as by members of the public through a competition organised by Crossrail.

Ada and Phyllis were named after Ada Lovelace, an early computer scientist and Phyllis Pearsall, who self-published the first London A–Z Map.

Victoria and Elizabeth were named after two monarchs. Queen Victoria ruled during the first great age of engineering while Her Majesty Elizabeth II was queen during the age of Crossrail.

Mary and Sophia were named after Mary Horsley, wife of the great civil engineer Isambard Kingdom Brunel, and his mother, Sophia Kingdom.

Jessica and Ellie were named after the track and field athlete Jessica Ennis-Hill and the swimmer Ellie Simmonds, who were gold medallists at the London 2012 Olympics and Paralympics.

TBM Victoria   ©Herrenknecht AG

A New Generation of Engineers

In 2011, Crossrail founded the Academy of Tunnelling and Construction to create the skilled workforce needed to construct the Elizabeth line and, as a longer term benefit to the country, it ensures the availability of a new generation of qualified tunnelling engineers and technicians. The academy (which has now merged with South Essex College) has so far trained more than 20,000 people.

Archaeology

The Crossrail construction sites created one of the UK's most extensive archaeological programmes. Over 100 archaeologists found tens of thousands of items spanning 55 million years of London's history and prehistory. Some of the more unusual finds include parts of the jawbone of a woolly mammoth, the largest piece of amber ever found in the UK, a pair of medieval ice skates, a bowling ball from the Tudor period and thousands of Victorian Crosse & Blackwell jam jars and pickle pots. In 2009, human and animal bones were found during borehole drilling in Farringdon. It was discovered that 682 victims of anthrax had been buried in that area in 1520. Crossrail immediately halted the excavations, as deadly anthrax spores can lie dormant for centuries and may be lethal if disturbed. However, the Health Protection Agency found no traces of anthrax or bubonic plague and tunnelling work was able to resume.

Sustainability

Energy-saving measures are incorporated in the stations themselves and in the design of the rolling stock, with features such as regenerative braking and intelligent lighting and temperature control as standard. There was also a landmark partnership with the Royal Society for the Protection of Birds. More than three million tonnes of excavated soil were taken by ship to Wallasea Island in Essex and used to create Jubilee Marsh, a new intertidal area of salt-marsh, islands and mudflats. The new marsh is a haven for local and migratory birds and also acts as an innovative flood defence scheme.

State of the Art Trains

A fleet of 70 Class 345 driver-operated trains runs on the Elizabeth line. The new trains were built in Derby by Alstom and created 760 jobs and 80 apprenticeships. Both during and after construction, the train systems underwent rigorous testing including simulations of extreme weather conditions. The 200-metre long trains, mostly configured as nine walk-through carriages, easily accommodate up to 1,500 passengers. Before the opening, safety tests were carried out, with volunteers taking part to check passenger flow and evacuation scenarios. The three sets of double doors along each carriage make it quicker and easier for passengers to get on and off the train. All trains will provide live travel information and free on-board wi-fi. On the outer section of the route, trains can reach speeds of 90mph.

Crossrail Trains at Paddington Station

Location of Walks

Key

1	Abbey Wood	13	Paddington
2	Tottenham Court Road	14	Custom House
3	Woolwich	15	Stratford
4	Iver	16	Hanwell
5	Bond Street	17	Slough
6	Hayes & Harlington	18	Reading
7	Canary Wharf	19	Taplow
8	Manor Park	20	Shenfield
9	Twyford	21	Harold Wood
10	Farringdon	22	Romford
11	Ealing Broadway	23	Maidenhead
12	Brentwood		

Walks by Distance

* walks with a shorter variant

Km	To the nearest half mile	Start and Finish Points	Walk	Page
4.5 km	3 miles	Abbey Wood Circular	1	10
5.5 km	3.5 miles	Tottenham Court Road to Farringdon	2	14
6.5 km	4 miles	Woolwich Circular	3	19
6.5 km	4 miles	Iver to West Drayton	4	23
6.5 km	4 miles	Bond Street to Paddington	5	26
7 km	4.5 miles	Hayes & Harlington to West Drayton	6	30
8 km	5 miles	Canary Wharf to Greenwich *	7	33
8 km	5 miles	Manor Park Circular	8	37
8 km	5 miles	Twyford Circular	9	41
8.5 km	5 miles	Farringdon to Whitechapel *	10	44
9 km	5.5 miles	Ealing Broadway to Hanwell	11	48
9 km	5.5 miles	Brentwood to Harold Wood	12	51
9 km	5.5 miles	Paddington to St Pancras *	13	55
9.5 km	6 miles	Custom House to Stratford	14	59
10 km	6 miles	Stratford to Canary Wharf	15	62
10 km	6 miles	Hanwell to Richmond	16	65
11 km	7 miles	Slough to Taplow	17	69
11 km	7 miles	Reading Circular *	18	73
11.5 km	7 miles	Taplow Circular *	19	76
12 km	7.5 miles	Shenfield to Brentwood *	20	80
14 km	9 miles	Harold Wood to Rainham*	21	84
14.5 km	9 miles	Romford to Harold Wood *	22	88
15.5 km	10 miles	Maidenhead to Marlow *	23	92

Lesnes Abbey Viewpoint

1 A Circular Walk from Abbey Wood through Lesnes Abbey Woods

Distance	4.5 km (3 miles)
Underfoot	Woodland and surfaced paths
Start	Abbey Wood Station (Elizabeth line; mainline)
Finish	Abbey Wood Station
Points of Interest	Lesnes Abbey ruins and garden; Lesnes Abbey Woods
Refreshments	Cafés at Abbey Wood Station and Lesnes Abbey Lodge
Toilets	Abbey Wood Station; Lesnes Abbey Lodge
Shortening the Walk	Green and yellow waymarked routes and other paths through the woods (see information boards)

Only 10 minutes from Abbey Wood Station, Lesnes Abbey and the surrounding woods form a green oasis with a panoramic view across the London skyline. This walk starts at the abbey ruins and is especially pleasant in spring when the trees turn green and the daffodils and bluebells are in flower. The route takes you through remnants of ancient forest and heathland on the hillsides through a mix of sweet chestnut, birch and oak. Although only 4.5 km long, there are several ups and downs through the woods, which make it an energetic undertaking. The woods are a local nature reserve and encompass several small ponds and a geological Site of Special Scientific Interest where fossils can be found. There are also several wooden sculptures to discover. For much of this walk you follow sections on the Green Chain Walk and the Lesnes Abbey 'Active' trail, waymarked in blue. There are two other waymarked routes (green and yellow) shown on the information board at the entrance.

Lesnes Abbey was founded in 1178 by Richard de Lucy, a trusted adviser to three kings: Henry I, Stephen and Henry II. Henry II appointed him as joint Chief Justiciar of England, making de Lucy one of the most powerful men in the country. When the king became embroiled in a bitter dispute with Thomas Becket, the Archbishop of Canterbury, de Lucy took the king's part and was then excommunicated by Becket, not just once but twice - an extreme and devastating punishment in an age when the fear of going to hell was very real. Despite the rumours, there is no firm evidence that de Lucy was one of the king's knights involved in Becket's murder in the cathedral at Canterbury in 1170. Becket was canonised three years later and Lesnes Abbey was dedicated by de Lucy not only to the Virgin Mary but also to St Thomas Becket. Canterbury soon became an extremely popular place of pilgrimage and pilgrims walking from London to Canterbury will have been offered food and lodging at the abbey en route. Richard de Lucy retired to the abbey in 1179 and lived simply as part of the Augustinian community until his death. The abbey never became wealthy, due to the expense of draining the marshes and maintaining the river banks. It was dissolved by Cardinal Wolsey in 1525 as it was no longer a viable monastic community.

1. Come out of the station and cross the road at the pedestrian lights. Turn right and walk over the flyover. At the end, turn left through an ornate metal entrance to Lesnes Abbey (one of the eight designed by Trish Hawes and forged by local metalsmith Heather Burrell). Follow the path for *Lesnes Abbey Ruins,* which rises up to reach a metal barrier. Go through and then turn left on a tarmac path with wooden fences on both sides, leading down to a road. Cross over and enter the Abbey grounds, going past a second ornate arch and a metal gate by an information board. To your right is a wooden statue of a monk, created by artist Tom Harvey, one of several of his sculptures in the woods.

2. At a fork, go right up steps to reach the Lodge (*toilets and refreshment kiosk*). Just past the lodge on the right is the entrance gate to the Monks' Garden (*worth a quick visit*). Turn left here by a yellow marker. Continue on this path, with the abbey ruins to your right, until you reach a round junction inlaid with a mosaic. Leave the tarmac path and go right on a gravel path past an old mulberry tree. Take the next path on the right up to the viewpoint with its three ecclesiastical metal windows, also the work of Heather Burrell. A panorama board identifies the places visible on the skyline, including the City and Canary Wharf.

3. Stay on the same path, ignoring a path to the right and another to the left, and go ahead into the woods. At a junction with a tall brown waymark pillar, turn left. You are now on the Green Chain Walk which goes up then down. Half way down, you pass the

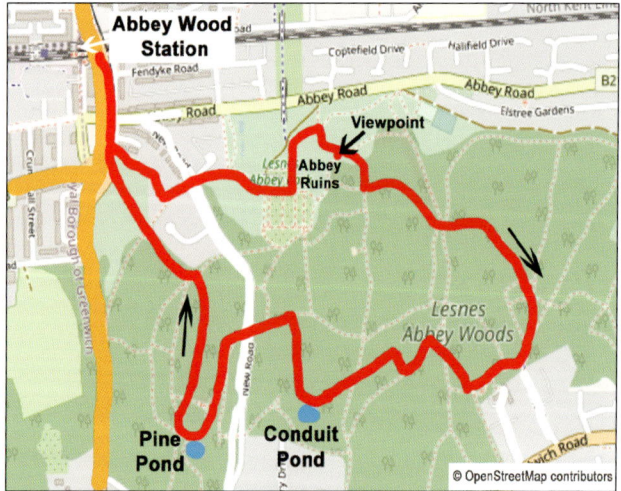

Green Man, a wooden carving. At a fork keep left and reach a crossing track by a second brown pillar and a Green Chain fingerpost. Go ahead on the *Green Chain Walk,* signposted for *Leather Bottle*.

4. The stepped path rises quite steeply and curves to the right. Just after passing a *Green Chain* sign, you reach an area of open heathland at the top of the hill, with an information board. The Green Chain Walk goes ahead here, but you go to the right, following an arrow on a blue marker post. Go right at the next blue marker, towards houses visible through the trees, passing the carved wooden seats of the Outdoor Classroom. Swing right at another blue marker post, just inside the boundary of the woods. Almost immediately, the path dips into a hollow. Turn right at its lowest point on a narrower path and walk steeply downhill for 130m. (*This avoids a steeper and, in wet weather, slippery section of the blue route*.) At the bottom, turn left for 200m to where the blue route comes in from the left by a marker post. Go ahead for 20m and turn right by a marker post onto a smaller path, which swings right. At another junction of paths, turn sharp left signposted *Conduit Pond* and walk uphill.

Lesnes Abbey ruins

Lesnes Abbey Woods

5. At a fork go right, following the blue marker post. At the top, go over a crossing path and walk downhill towards another post. Keep left here to reach Conduit Pond. Continue past the pond on a path that climbs and swings right. In 50m, ignore a path to the left and continue in the same direction, ignoring another path to the left as you go along the ridge. When you reach a fork, you can see down to your right the *Data Tree,* a community art project inspired by artist Jonathan Wright. You, however, fork left and go downhill to reach a T-junction and a marker post. Turn left downhill onto a broad track. You soon arrive at a road. Cross over with care and follow a *Green Chain* sign onto the footpath directly opposite. The path goes left and later swings to the right. Continue to climb for 200m until you reach a small pond. Continue ahead, with the pond on your right, for 70m to reach the attractive Pine Pond. Turn right in front of the pond by a *Green Chain Walk* marker, towards another marker post visible ahead. Leave the Green Chain and the blue route here and take the path immediately on the right going slightly downhill. Continue over a crossing path. The path now goes along fairly level for 100m but then starts to descend. Keep left where a path comes in from the right and descend more steeply, with housing visible ahead through the trees.

6. When you reach a T-junction, ignore the arrow on the marker post pointing to the right, back towards Lesnes Abbey. Instead, to finish the walk, turn left. Follow the track downhill, keeping the houses on your right. Ignore a succession of paths which come in from your left. After 200m, climb a short uphill stretch to reach a large sunken track that cuts across your route. Go straight over the track and up the short bank opposite to emerge by a signpost at the top of a meadow. There is a clear view of your starting-point below. Go down across the grass and back over the flyover to Abbey Wood Station.

Green Man

Fountain Court, Middle Temple

2 Tottenham Court Road to Farringdon: Hidden Alleyways, Squares and Gardens

Distance	**5.5 km (3.5 miles)**
Underfoot	**Paved surfaces throughout**
Start	**Tottenham Court Road Station (Elizabeth line; London Underground)**
Finish	**Farringdon Station (Elizabeth line; mainline; London Underground)**
Points of Interest	**Soho Square; Phoenix Garden; Seven Dials; Covent Garden; Lincoln's Inn Fields; Inns of Court; Temple Church; Dr Johnson's House**
Refreshments	**Many opportunities en route**
Toilets	**Covent Garden; Lincoln's Inn Fields**
Shortening the Walk	**The walk crosses several bus routes**

This walk follows hidden alleyways, gardens and squares, avoiding busy streets wherever possible. You go past the Church of St Giles-in-the-Fields and the secluded Phoenix Garden before reaching Covent Garden. The walk continues to Lincoln's Inn Fields and explores the precincts of three of London's Inns of Court: Lincoln's Inn, Middle Temple and Inner Temple. Entering the alleyways to the north of Fleet Street you find No. 17 Gough Square, where Dr Samuel Johnson lived. Finally the walk passes beneath Holborn Viaduct to reach Farringdon Station. Please note that at weekends and on Bank Holidays Lincoln's Inn is closed to the public. Access routes to the Middle and Inner Temple are also more limited. If you are doing this route at a weekend, please follow the suggested diversions.

1. Leave the Elizabeth line station by the western exit on Dean Street. Turn right, away from Oxford Street. Take the first left into Carlisle Street and Soho Square. (*If you leave the station via a different exit, walk west along Oxford Street and turn left into Soho Street to reach Soho Square.*) Leave the square in the far corner by the House of Charity and enter Greek Street. Take the first left into Manette Street and go past the tiny Church of St Barnabas. Cross over Charing Cross Road at the lights that are slightly to your left. Turn right and then take a narrow lane, Flitcroft Street, to the left beside the Phoenix Theatre. Walk up to Denmark Street and then turn right into the churchyard of St Giles-in-the-Fields.

2. Walk to the right of the church, then turn left and right, with a playground and the Phoenix Garden on your right. Go ahead on St Giles Passage. Cross straight over New Compton Street and

Shaftesbury Avenue. Continue ahead on Mercer Street. At the Seven Dials monument, take the third exit on the left into Earlham Street, next to the Cambridge Theatre. At the end, turn right into Neal Street and continue to its junction with Long Acre. Cross at the zebra crossing and continue down James Street to reach Covent Garden (*toilets and refreshments*). Turn left to walk beneath the colonnade that leads up to the Royal Opera House. Go right at the opera house and then turn left to walk along Russell Street. Cross Bow Street and Drury Lane, past some well-known theatres. Continue ahead along Kemble Street, which swings to

Covent Garden

15

the right to reach Kingsway. Go left for 100m in order to cross the dual carriageway at the lights. Turn right and then left into Sardinia Street by the London School of Economics.

3. Cross over at a zebra crossing and enter Lincoln's Inn Fields through the gate on the corner. Turn left and then right through the centre of the park towards a round shelter. Continue ahead and leave the park opposite Lincoln's Inn (*public toilets to the left here*). Cross over and turn right, with a view of the spire of the Royal Courts of Justice ahead. Enter Lincoln's Inn by the gate on the left. New Square is on your right. Go ahead and take the

Weekends and Bank Holidays: The paths of the Inns of Court are not public rights of way and access may not always be possible. At weekends and on Bank Holidays there is no public access at all to Lincoln's Inn. While there is access to Inner Temple and Middle Temple, not all the gates are open. Please see the alternative routes.

first path to the left alongside the Great Hall and Library. Turn right in front of Stone Buildings to enter Old Square. Turn right towards the chapel and go through an archway into the vaulted area. Exit to the right through the arch between the twin staircases that lead up to the chapel (*open to the public*). Go left and right to return to New Square. Turn left to walk along its length, with the gardens on your right, and exit through the ornate archway ahead into Carey Street.

If the entrance to Lincoln's Inn is closed continue down Serle Street and turn left into Carey Street. Rejoin the main walk at Bell Yard.

4. Turn left and take the next right into Bell Yard, alongside the Royal Courts of Justice. Turn right into The Strand. Walk past Temple Bar Memorial and the Royal Courts of Justice. Cross over the Strand at the first of two zebra crossings and turn right. After 40m, go left into a narrow alleyway, Devereux Court. Follow the alleyway going left then right till you see on your left the

New Square, Lincoln's Inn

entrance to the Temple area (Gate 4). Go through into New Court, then turn right to reach Fountain Court.

If Gate 4 into the Temple is closed, stay on Devereux Alley as it goes right. Take the first left into Essex Road. Go down the steps at the end into Milford Lane. Keep ahead to reach Victoria Embankment. Turn left, following the railings of the Temple gardens.

Take the first left into Temple Avenue and first left into Tudor Road. Enter the Temple precincts. Turn right along King's Bench Walk. Go left through a passageway just after Temple Library to reach the Temple Church. Go ahead through another passageway into Pump Court and exit on the opposite side into Middle Temple Lane.

Turn left, then immediately right into Fountain Court. Turn left into Garden Court to view Middle Temple Garden. Retrace your steps to Middle Temple Lane. Turn right. Take the first left, Crown Office Row, to King's Bench Walk. Exit onto Tudor Street via the gate you came in by. Go past Temple Lane and take the next left into Bouverie Street. Rejoin the main walk at Fleet Street.

5. Continue past the fountain into Garden Court, with views of Middle Temple Garden ahead (*open to the public at certain times*). Swing to the right down some steps and leave the Middle Temple through a gate leading onto Milford Lane. Turn left and then left again when you reach the Victoria Embankment. Go past Middle Temple garden and enter the Temple area again through the Embankment gate. Continue ahead through the arch into Middle Temple Lane. You soon reach Fountain Court again, on the opposite side to before. Turn right here by the

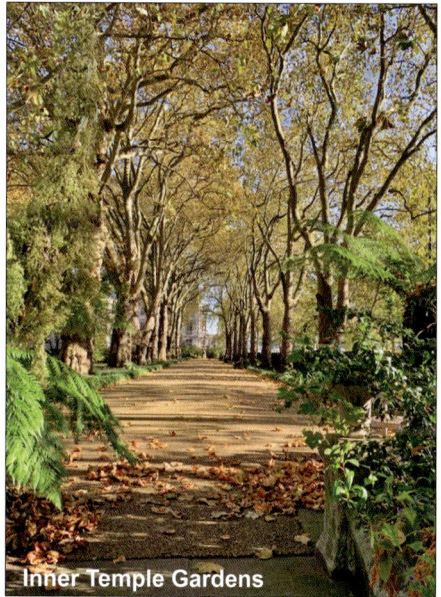
Inner Temple Gardens

Lamb Building through a passageway, following signs for the *Inner Temple* and *Temple Church*. Keep left through Elm Court and climb the steps in the corner. Go through the cloister arches to arrive at Temple Church.

6. Walk to the right of the church and go through a passageway into King's Bench Walk. Turn left and go through an arch under Mitre Court Buildings to Serjeants' Inn Courtyard. Turn right and leave via a passageway, next to a hotel, which leads to Lombard Lane. Turn left, then turn right into Pleydell Street, and left into Bouverie Street. Cross Fleet Street at the set of lights to your right. (*A short detour to the right here would lead you to the historic Cheshire Cheese pub.*) Go ahead into Bolt Court. Swing right and then left to reach Gough Square with its 'talking' memorial to Hodge, Dr Johnson's cat. Johnson's House and Museum is to your left. Go right into Gunpowder Square, then ahead on Wine Office

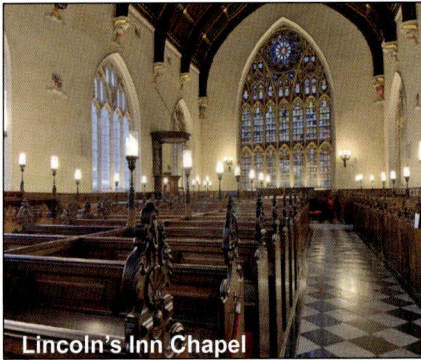
Lincoln's Inn Chapel

Court. Turn left into Shoe Lane. At a five-way crossroads continue on Shoe Lane on a walkway that swings right past the Goldman Sachs building. Still on Shoe Lane, go under Holborn Viaduct, then turn right on Charterhouse Street. Cross over and go down the steps into Saffron Hill, just to the left of the lights. At the first crossroads, turn right into Greville Street. Continue ahead to the lights on Farringdon Road and cross over to reach the Elizabeth line station.

Phoenix Garden is a community garden created on a former WW2 bombsite. Its sheltered position allows plants from more temperate climates to thrive. Run by volunteers, the garden is open to the public daily.

Covent Garden was once London's major fruit, vegetable and flower market. Its neo-classical buildings date from 1830, though the market itself is much older. Covent Garden Piazza opened in its present form in 1980 after the relocation of the fruit and vegetable market. It is a lively venue with street performers and classical musicians, boutiques, craft stalls, restaurants and the Jubilee Market. The area is also home to the London Transport Museum, the Royal Opera House and St Paul's Church, often referred to as the Actors' Church.

The Inns of Court were set up in London to cater for the education of the class of professional lawyers emerging from the late 13th century. Four remain today: Lincoln's Inn, Inner Temple, Middle Temple and Gray's Inn. The Inns still provide legal education and have the exclusive right to call practitioners to the Bar. Many of the buildings are Grade I listed and set in beautiful grounds. Visitors are welcome to explore the precincts of the Inns of Court but, with the exception of the chapels, the buildings themselves are not generally open to the public. The Inner and Middle Temple gardens are open at certain times.

Temple Church was built by the Knights Templar, a powerful monastic order of crusaders who protected pilgrims to the Holy Land. It was consecrated in 1185 by the Patriarch of Jerusalem. The design of the Round Church is based on the Church of the Holy Sepulchre in Jerusalem. The Chancel was added in 1240. Temple Church has been in the care of Inner and Middle Temple for 400 years. Visitors are welcome (*admission charge*).

Dr Johnson's House is a 300-year-old Grade I-listed building, tucked away in a corner of Gough Square amongst a maze of courts and alleyways. Now a museum, it was home to Samuel Johnson (1709-84) who came to London as a teacher seeking his fortune. He established himself as a poet, playwright, essayist and moralist. A sociable man with a wide circle of friends, he is quoted as saying: '*When a man is tired of London, he is tired of life*'. He is perhaps best known for his *Dictionary of the English Language*, published in 1755.

Thames Path at Woolwich

3 A Circular Walk from Woolwich along the Thames Path: Climb the Highest Peak in Thamesmead

Distance	**6.5 km (4 miles)**
Underfoot	**Paved surfaces and gravel paths**
Start	**Woolwich Station (Elizabeth line)**
Finish	**Woolwich Station; Woolwich Arsenal Station**
Points of Interest	**Royal Arsenal Heritage Area; Thames Path; Broadwater; Gallions Park; Gallions Hill**
Refreshments	**Pubs; café; M&S Foodhall, all near Dial Arch Square**
Toilets	**Beresford Square, next to the Royal Arsenal Gatehouse**
Shortening the Walk	**Leave out the climb to the top of Gallions Hill**

This easy circular walk is full of interesting sights and experiences. Woolwich Station is in Woolwich Riverside, a short distance from Woolwich town centre and the mainline station. A recent regeneration project has seen new housing built along the bank of the Thames and also the careful conversion of historic buildings of the former Royal Arsenal into a mixed use area. The walk starts and finishes in the Woolwich Heritage conservation area, going past the foundries, factories, warehouses and military buildings where ammunition, weapons and explosives were manufactured and research undertaken for over 300 years. In between, there is a lovely walk along the Thames Path, passing remnants of a former canal and climbing an unusual manmade hill.

Royal Arsenal Heritage Area

You exit **Woolwich Station** directly onto Dial Arch Square. The walk starts by taking you round the perimeter of the square, passing many listed buildings, and then continues down No.1 Street to reach the Thames.

Turn left out of the station. Ahead of you, across the main road, is the original **Royal Arsenal Gatehouse**, built in 1828. The gatehouse had three openings: the middle one for horses and carriages, the narrower outside ones for pedestrians. Cross the the road only if you want a closer look or to use the public toilets to the right of the Gatehouse. Otherwise, turn right in front of **Verbruggen's House**, built in 1772-3 for the two Dutch master founders who took over the running of the brass foundry.

Ahead is the **Main Guardhouse** on No.1 Street, built in 1788, now a pub/restaurant. In front of its classical portico is a sculpture representing Nike, the personification of victory in Greek mythology, a gift from the city of Olympia to commemorate the 2012 Olympic Games. Turn right down No.1 Street.

Next on the left is the **Royal Brass Foundry**, built in 1717. The tall doors were designed to allow the easy transport of the cannon cast here.

On the other side of the road is the **Dial Arch** building, now a pub/restaurant, at the head of the green space outside the Crossrail station. The arch is named after the sundial in the wall, dating from 1764. The quadrangle of the building was where the brass cannon from the foundry were brought for finishing.

1. Continue down No. 1 Street, soon passing Artillery Square on your left, with the former Royal Military Academy on the opposite side. The Academy opened here in 1741, but relocated to Woolwich Common in 1806. Continue ahead to James Clavell Square and *Assembly*, an artwork by Peter Burke, with 16 cast-iron figures in a circle, installed here in 2005. Go up the steps to the right, towards Woolwich Pier. The two hexagonal buildings to the left are the former guardhouses of the Royal Arsenal river entrance. Turn right and walk along the Thames Path. After 400m turn right, left and left again round a water inlet by a green-roofed DLR ventilation shaft. Do not go all the way down to the riverside path. Instead, stay at a

Royal Brass Foundry

higher level by following a sign for *Quietway Q14* and *Thamesmead* to the right, on a footpath next to the cycleway.

2. After 600m, shortly before a row of houses, you go past Broadwater Lock, behind a double set of metal railings. Go past the first block of houses and turn right towards parkland on a signposted joint footpath and cycle path. When you come to a railing by a basketball court, take the path to the right to reach Broadwater, all that remains of the former Royal Arsenal Canal. Turn left to walk beside the water, but just before you reach more houses, turn left away from the old canal towards Warepoint Drive. Cross over by a bus stop and go into Gallions Park. Turn right at the first path you come to (just past some steps) and follow it as it makes its way down to reach the lake. Walk along the lakeside past several benches. Where the asphalt ends, go left up some steps and turn right on a path to continue walking alongside the water.

3. Ignore a footbridge to the right and continue up to a crossing road. Go straight over and continue ahead in the same direction, by a signpost for *Foxglove Path 210yds*, to the right of a residential road. Take the lower of two

Broadwater: the remains of the Royal Arsenal Canal

paths, along the bank of a small river. Stay on this path, ignoring another pedestrian bridge over the river. When you arrive at a row of houses, turn right on Foxglove Path, with the river still on your right. Leave the path at the second road on your left, Longmarsh Lane, to reach the base of Gallions Hill, which was created from soil excavated when the surrounding housing was built. Cross the road and turn right to reach the pedestrian access to Gallions Hill. Go past the barrier onto a footpath. After 50m you come to the entrance to Gallions Reach Play Area on your right, which you will return to later. Follow the spiral path to the top of Gallions Hill, a distance of 500m each way. (*To shorten the walk, you can leave out the climb up the hill and go straight through the play area.*) From the summit of the hill there is an all-round view of the surrounding area. You may also enjoy watching the planes coming in to land or taking off at nearby City Airport.

4. After walking back down, return to the play area you passed earlier. Walk through it, then follow the path as it winds along between grass-covered mounds. At the end of the park, go ahead down some steps to rejoin the Thames Path. Turn left here and stay on the lower level path until you reach the inlet by the DLR ventilation shaft again. Go up a ramp and steps and turn right at the top. On a level with the ventilation shaft, turn left away from the river, through a car parking area, to reach Cadogan Road, with Cannon House opposite. Turn right, and then take the third road on the left, Arsenal Way, after passing the former Grand Store on your right and Wellington Park on your left. You pass the gatehouse of the former Shell Foundry with two historic cannon in front of the entrance. Take the first right, Duke of Wellington Avenue. Go past the former carriage works, then take the next left into Major Draper Street, which leads back to Woolwich Station.

Woolwich Station is one of 10 new stations on the Elizabeth line. The entrance opens out directly onto Dial Arch Square with its many listed buildings. The design of the station makes reference to the military history of the area, with the cladding reflecting the patterns caused by rifling within the barrel of an artillery piece. The decorative motif on the mesh above the station entrance features an exploded view of the First World War 'dead man's penny', a medal given to families of the fallen. The colours on the interior columns reflect the regimental colours of the two artillery companies based in Woolwich Royal Arsenal.

Dial Square Football Team was created in 1886 by Royal Arsenal workers who took as their team name the playing area located in front of the Dial Arch. Later, when they turned professional in 1891, the club became known as Woolwich Arsenal. When the club moved to Highbury in North London in 1913 it became Arsenal FC.

Broadwater Lock sits at the entrance of the former Royal Arsenal Canal, built between 1812 and 1816 by French prisoners of war and convicts who were housed in hulks moored in Woolwich Reach. The canal was originally used to take goods between the Thames and the Royal Arsenal. It served an early 19th century sawmill and also acted as a defensive boundary. In the 1960s, when the Royal Arsenal ceased production, the canal fell into disuse and the lock was closed.

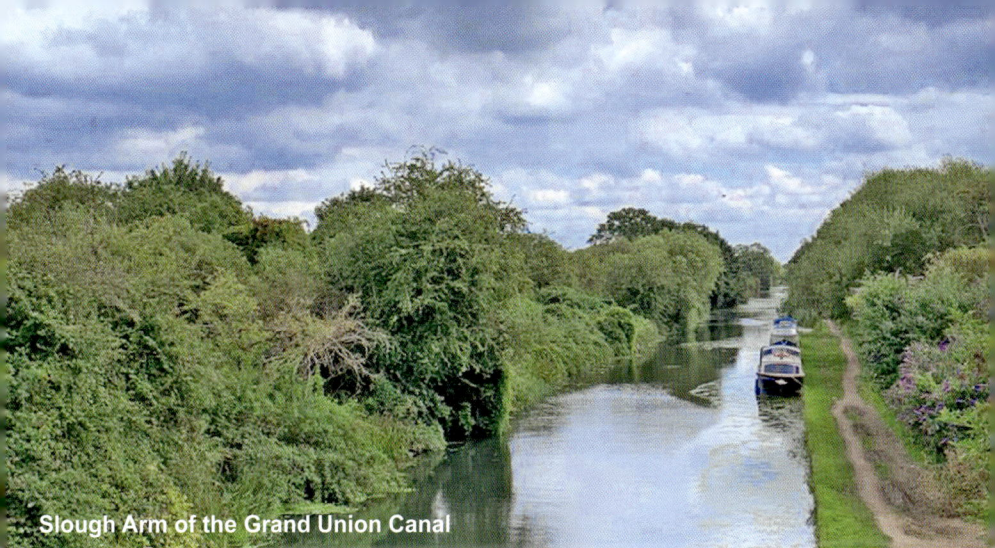

Slough Arm of the Grand Union Canal

4 Iver to West Drayton via the River Colne and the Grand Union Canal

Distance	**6.5 km (4 miles)**
Underfoot	**Towpaths and riverside paths, a few stretches muddy in winter and after heavy rain**
Start	**Iver Station (Elizabeth line)**
Finish	**West Drayton (Elizabeth line; mainline)**
Points of Interest	**Grand Union Canal; Little Britain Lake; River Colne; Cowley Lock**
Refreshments	**Two canalside pubs**
Toilets	**At Iver and West Drayton Stations**
Shortening the Walk	**No options**

This is a lovely walk exploring three waterways and a lake between two Crossrail stations. It includes stretches on the London Loop through the Colne Valley Park and towpath walks along the Grand Union Canal. The first waterside section is the Slough Arm of the Grand Union Canal. During this stretch you cross two aqueducts over the Colne Brook and the River Colne. An easy footpath leads to the delightful Little Britain Lake, a haven for birds including swans, herons and great crested grebes, as well as wildfowl migrants. Next comes a picturesque stroll along the banks of the River Colne. Finally, you follow the towpath of the main Grand Union Canal for 2.5 km, passing many moored narrowboats and two canalside pubs before reaching West Drayton.

1. Come out of Iver Station and turn back left alongside the glass wall of the station to walk along the footpath that runs beside the railway line. At a road (Thorney Lane North) turn left. Walk along the footway for 600m, passing a sign for Iver Village. You will see a bridge ahead with a traffic light at the far end. Cross over to the right-hand side of the road and just before reaching the bridge, turn right onto a path by a public footpath sign and an information board for the Slough Arm of the Grand Union Canal. The path slopes gently down to join the canal. Continue along the towpath in the same direction, soon passing under a motorway bridge (M25).

2. During this stretch of canal walking there are two aqueducts to cross, the first over the Colne Brook and the second over the River Colne. After 1km you reach a metal footbridge, with a path next to it going up to the right, by a large white stone marker. Leave the towpath here and go up to

West Drayton

a track with a wooden fingerpost for the *Colne Valley Trail* and the *London Loop*. Go left here over the bridge and continue on the gravel track that winds between the trees. After 300m, by some parking bays and an access road, you reach the attractive Little Britain Lake. There are footpath signs and an information board here.

3. Go to the left of the lake, following the signs for the *London Loop* and *Trails of Discovery*. Just a few metres further on, there is a viewing platform on your right. Almost immediately after this, go left to cross a footbridge over the River Colne. Turn right and follow the *London Loop* sign and follow this path for over 1km through the woods, with views of the river on your right. (*Expect a few muddy stretches in the winter.*)

4. When you reach a road (Iver Lane), cross over and turn right. Shortly before a *Welcome to Cowley* sign, the London Loop goes off to the left. You, however, continue ahead on the road to a humpback bridge. Go over the bridge, carefully cross the road and go down to the Grand Union Canal in front

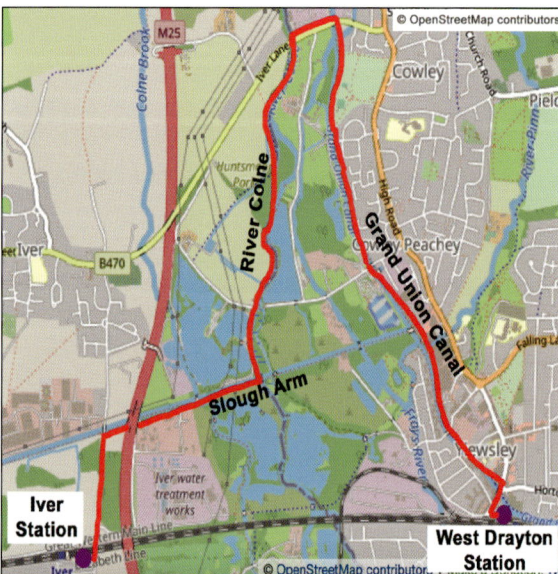

of the Malt Shovel pub. Go ahead past Cowley Lock and stay on the towpath all the way for the final 2.5 km to West Drayton. You pass another canalside pub, The Watersedge, on the opposite bank (*accessible by a bridge*) and many moored narrowboats and modern apartment buildings. After passing under the old brick canal bridge at Trout Road, you see ahead of you the visually striking steel arches of a road bridge. When you reach this bridge, go under it and then leave the canal by the ramp that takes you up to street level. Turn left across the bridge and then left again into Station Approach to reach West Drayton Station.

The Slough Arm is one of the many arms of the Grand Union Canal and the most recent one. At 8 km it is also one of the shortest, linking Cowley Peachey Junction with Slough. It opened in 1882 to serve the local brick-making industry. Several wharves for bricks, gravel and sand were created along it. It has three aqueducts but no locks. The final commercial cargo journey was made in 1960 and the local council developed plans to create a road where the canal had been. The proposal was successfully challenged by the Slough Canal Group and it re-opened in 1975 for recreational use.

Canalside pubs were an essential part of canal life, providing food and rest for the boatmen, their families and their horses. Some inns catered for the needs of the leggers, who navigated the boats through the tunnels in the 18th and 19th centuries. Others would provide stabling and replacement horses for the barges.

The River Colne rises in Hertfordshire and flows south for 62 km (39 miles) to join the Thames at Staines. The section in this walk forms the boundary between Buckinghamshire and Greater London. Little Britain Lake, so-called because of its shape, is one of many lakes along the lower course of the River Colne south of Rickmansworth. Created by the flooding of former gravel and clay pits, they are important habitats for wildlife.

Little Britain Lake

Green Park

5   Bond Street to Paddington via Grosvenor Square, Green Park and Hyde Park

Distance	6.5 km (4 miles)
Underfoot	Mostly paved surfaces
Start	Davies Street exit at Bond Street Station (Elizabeth line; London Underground)
Finish	Paddington (Elizabeth line; Underground; mainline)
Points of Interest	Grosvenor Square; Mount Street Gardens; Berkeley Square; Green Park; Hyde Park; The Serpentine; Diana Fountain; Kensington Gardens; Italian Gardens
Refreshments	Many opportunities en route
Toilets	Green Park Underground Station; Hyde Park; Kensington Gardens
Shortening the Walk	Take a bus from Hyde Park Corner back to Bond Street

This is a city walk with an abundance of green spaces and interesting sights. It starts near Oxford Street and makes its way through the smart streets of Mayfair, visiting Grosvenor Square, Mount Street Gardens and Berkeley Square before entering Green Park, passing close to Buckingham Palace. Next comes Hyde Park, with a walk through the rose garden and around the Serpentine, past the Diana Memorial Fountain. In Kensington Gardens the route continues along the water, passing the statue of Peter Pan before arriving at the Italian Gardens. You leave the park at Lancaster Gate, only 600m from Paddington Station.

1. Leave Bond Street Station by the Davies Street exit and turn right. Take the second road on the right, Brook Street. Walk for 150m until you reach Grosvenor Square, cross at the zebra crossings and enter the tree-lined square. There are several memorials here linked to the United States of America. To your left is a pergola dedicated to the lives lost in the 9/11 attack on the Twin Towers in New York in 2001. Walk diagonally across the park, passing the statue of Roosevelt (to the right of the centre) and the Eagle Squadrons Memorial (to the left).

2. Exit at the far left corner and cross over to enter South Audley Street opposite. Go ahead at the traffic lights at the junction with Mount Street, then take the first left, immediately before a church, into a short cul-de-sac which leads into Mount Street Gardens. The gardens, which were first created in the 19th century, are a haven of peace and quiet in the heart of Mayfair. Take time to marvel at the huge palm tree and read a few of the dedications on the benches. Exit at the far end of the gardens past the Catholic church. Turn right into Mount Street opposite the Connaught Hotel and the *Silence* fountain.

3. Walk for 150m to a T-junction and turn right into Davies Street. Turn left at Berkeley Square and then cross over to enter the gardens through the gate at the top of the square. Walk down through the centre of the square. The large plane trees planted here in 1789 are some of the oldest in London. Leave the square at the far end. Your onward route is to the left, but to cross safely, use the zebra crossing to your right, then turn back and swing right into Berkeley Street. Continue ahead until you reach a T-junction with Piccadilly. Facing you is the Ritz Hotel. Cross at the traffic lights, turn right for 25m and then left

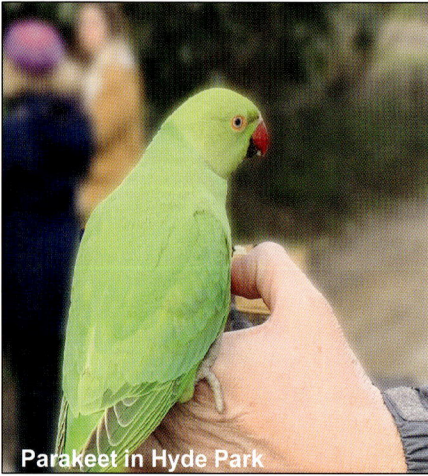
Parakeet in Hyde Park

Park Corner and the Wellington Arch, which was built to commemorate Britain's victories in the Napoleonic Wars in the early 19th century. Go through the arch and walk to the top right-hand corner of the centre island. Cross over at two sets of traffic lights and enter Hyde Park through the monumental entrance designed by Decimus Burton in 1825. Cross South Carriage Drive and turn left along Rotten Row, following a signpost for *Kensington Gardens.* To your right you can see the decorative gates erected in honour of the 90th birthday of Elizabeth, the Queen Mother.

into Queen's Walk, which runs down the left-hand side of Green Park.

4. After 50m turn right and walk to a circular junction of paths. (*There are toilets in Green Park Station to your right.*) There are various pleasant routes through the park, either on paths or simply straight across the grass. The quickest onward route is to go straight on along the top of Green Park on a path parallel to Piccadilly. After passing the Bomber Command Memorial, turn left beside a hedge to reach a set of pedestrian lights. Cross over here to the central island of Hyde

5. After 50m leave Rotten Row and go half-right by a *Princess of Wales Memorial Walk* plaque to enter the Rose Garden. Leave the garden and keep ahead on the same path until it swings right and goes up towards a waterside café. Turn sharp left along the back of the café to reach the Serpentine. Follow this path along the waterfront, with the lake on your right, passing the lido, a café and toilets after 300m. Continue past the Diana Fountain on your left. Just after the entrance to the fountain, keep right at a fork in the path and go under a bridge to enter Kensington

Horseguards near Buckingham Palace

Gardens, with the Long Water to your right. Over to your left is the Serpentine Art Gallery. You may see green parakeets on this stretch. Follow the path past the Peter Pan monument and arrive at the Italian Gardens at the end of the lake. This ornamental water garden with its many pools, fountains and statues was a gift to Queen Victoria from Prince Albert in 1860.

6. Go past the ornate Pump House and leave the park by the exit to the left of a café and toilets. Cross at the lights and walk ahead on the left-hand footway to the junction with the A402. Cross carefully via a paved triangle to Sussex Gardens. Keep to the right of the park

Berkeley Square

railings, cross at the lights to another triangle and use the zebra crossing to continue ahead on the left-hand footway. Take the next left into Spring Street and walk to the junction with Praed Street. Ahead of you on the opposite side of the road is the Elizabeth line station at Paddington.

Green Park was developed as a Royal Park by Charles II in the 17th century. It was often used by Charles and successive monarchs as a venue for entertaining guests. In 1749, George II commissioned Handel's *Music for the Royal Fireworks*, which was to be performed in the park as part of a celebration of the end of the War of the Austrian Succession. The music proved tremendously popular, but the event ended in chaos when a stray firework set a woman's dress alight, another blinded one man and injured two soldiers and a third set fire to the structure housing the fireworks. The park today is unusual in that unlike other Royal Parks in London it has no lake, buildings or formal gardens, only a magnificent display of daffodils in spring.

Hyde Park is another of the eight Royal Parks in London and offers tranquil spaces as well as being a world-class concert venue. Apart from its recreational value, it has traditionally been a site for protests and marches and Speakers' Corner on a Sunday brings people from all walks of life to come and share their views.

Diana Princess of Wales Memorial Fountain is an oval granite loop where different effects are created in the water, which flows in two directions before coming to rest in a large tranquil pool. Opened by Queen Elizabeth II in July 2004, the fountain was initially beset by technical problems, but has now become a much-loved attraction.

The Serpentine was created in the 18th century by damming the River Westbourne. It was one of the earliest 'natural' artificial lakes, a feature widely replicated in parks and gardens nationwide. Since 2012, the water of the lake has been supplied by three boreholes in the chalk aquifer beneath the park. There are two art galleries close by.

Grand Union Canal near Hayes & Harlington

6 Hayes & Harlington to West Drayton via the Grand Union Canal and Stockley Park

Distance	7 km (4.5 miles)
Underfoot	Mostly towpaths and firm parkland paths
Start	Hayes & Harlington (Elizabeth line; mainline)
Finish	West Drayton (Elizabeth line; mainline)
Points of Interest	Grand Union Canal; Lake Farm Country Park; Stockley Country Park
Refreshments	Café and restaurant at the golf club in Stockley Pines
Toilets	Hayes & Harlington and West Drayton Stations
Shortening the Walk	No options

This walk starts and finishes with two stretches of easy towpath walking along the Grand Union Canal. In between, it crosses two country parks and passes a modern landscaped business centre and a golf course. After the first stretch along the canal, you enter Lake Farm Country Park and walk its entire length from south to north. You then turn south again and head towards Stockley Park Business Park, known to all football fans as the home of VAR. You pass through an almost hidden gateway into Stockley Country Park where the route soon joins the London Loop, which it follows over a pedestrian bridge above the A408 to a viewpoint, before turning downhill through woodland. The walk makes its way back to the Grand Union Canal along a section of newly constructed heritage path and reaches West Drayton Station via the towpath.

1. Turn right out of the station. You soon reach a bridge over the Grand Union Canal. Cross the bridge and take the steps to the right to join the towpath. Go under the bridge. You might spot an old metal canal sign which states *Braunston 87 miles*. After 550m you go under a road bridge. 350m after this, leave the towpath through a green metal gate into Lake Farm Country Park, following a sign for *Trails of Discovery*.

2. Go left at the fork and then swing right. Stay on this path, ignoring smaller paths to the left and right until you reach a T-junction, shortly after a bench. Turn right here. At a junction, cross straight over onto a broad path. Continue ahead, soon passing a BMX track and then a skateboard park. After this, take the next path to the left, which goes diagonally towards the top left-hand corner of the park. Leave the park. You come out onto a side road, just before its junction with Dawley Road. Turn left into Dawley Road and follow the footway to the right of the park perimeter fence.

3. When you reach a traffic island, cross to the other side of this busy road and continue until you come to

Bolingbroke Way. Turn right here and walk down towards a junction in front of Stockley Park business park. Just before reaching it, look out for a black metal swing gate in the railings to your right, partly hidden by ivy. Go through the gate onto a narrow path through trees. Shortly after, turn left on a broader path which goes round the perimeter of the golf course, with the buildings of the business park on your left. A few metres before you reach a road, by a large glass building, stay on the broad path as it swings right, ignoring a narrow path to the right that leads onto the golf course.

4. The path divides into two parallel tracks. The narrower right-hand one has a *London Loop* sign. Take either, as they join up later, shortly before a large overspill car parking area. The London Loop swings left to go round the parking area, but in wet weather you might choose to go straight ahead on a firm path. At the end of the car park, go ahead on the road for a short way till you come to a *London Loop* signpost. Turn right here, signposted for *West Drayton*, going past the golf club bar and The Orangery restaurant (*both open to the general public*). Ignore the turning to the left up to the

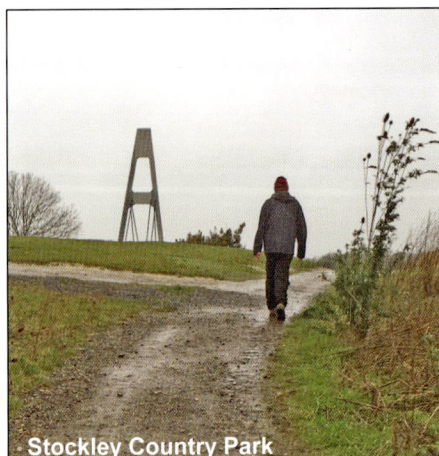
Stockley Country Park

1st tee and continue ahead uphill. You soon see the tall concrete arch of a bridge on the brow of the hill. Join a golf course track and go left to cross the bridge over a dual carriageway.

5. 75m after the bridge, just after a *London Loop* and a *321* sign, go to the right up a grassy path to the top of a small hillock to a viewpoint with all-round views. From the top of the hill, go down the grass path on the left to reach the path you were on previously. Cross straight over it and go downhill, following a dilapidated *London Loop* marker. Keep left at a fork. At the next fork, by a *London Loop* sign, take the narrower path to the right. At a third fork, keep right again towards a gate and exit onto the road by a bus stop. Cross the road and go ahead into Weston Walk. When you reach an ornamental mound by an information board, go down the steps to the right to rejoin the canal. Turn right and continue along the towpath, passing another metal sign showing the distance to Braunston. Shortly after going under a bridge, you see West Drayton Station on the opposite side of the canal. Walk on to the next bridge with its distinctive arches and turn right up a ramp to leave the towpath. Turn left to go over the canal and take the first left to reach the station.

Brickmaking in West Drayton was dependent on the clay soil you meet underfoot on this walk. There are records of a brickfield here in the 16th century, but the industry did not fully develop until the 19th century, when the local clay was much in demand for the yellow stock bricks of Victorian London. Brickmaking became one of the biggest occupations in West Drayton and neighbouring Stockley, Cowley and Yiewsley. An extension of the Grand Junction Canal was built in the 1870s to serve the industry, with each barge able to carry 13,000 bricks. By 1885 it is thought that one in 10 of the parishioners in West Drayton were working in the brickfields and by the 1890s an estimated 100 million bricks were being produced in the area each year. The work was seasonal and poorly paid and strikes were threatened in the 1890s, as workers became unionised. By the start of the 20th century, the supply of brick-earth was much depleted and the brickfields went into decline. Follow-on industries developed around gravel and sand extraction and the Grand Union Canal barges continued to serve these industries until the 1960s.

Stockley Park takes its name from a former brickworks. In 1986 the UK's first business park opened here within a country park which also provides outdoor leisure facilities and a golf course. Underpinned by a philosophy of sustainability, the landscape has been designed to include various wildlife habitats and areas of woodland. The Premier League's video assistant referee (VAR) operates from Stockley Park.

Old Royal Naval College

7 Canary Wharf to the World Heritage Site of Maritime Greenwich

Distance	**8 km (5 miles)**
Underfoot	**Mostly paved surfaces**
Start	**Canary Wharf Elizabeth Line Station**
Finish	**Greenwich Cutty Sark DLR Station to West India Quay (for Canary Wharf); Greenwich Station (mainline; DLR)**
Points of Interest	**Canary Wharf; Thames Foot Tunnel; *Cutty Sark*; Royal Naval College; Greenwich Park; Royal Observatory; Prime Meridian; Greenwich Market**
Refreshments	**Many opportunities in Canary Wharf and Greenwich**
Toilets	**Crossrail Place Level -3; Jubilee Place; Greenwich Visitor Centre; Greenwich Park**
Shortening the Walk	**Return from Island Gardens DLR Station**

This walk is full of interest and Maritime Greenwich boasts many sites of historical importance. After following the docksides and walkways of Canary Wharf, the route crosses Mudchute Park, goes through the Greenwich Foot Tunnel and emerges on the south bank of the Thames beside the *Cutty Sark*, the world's only remaining tea clipper. The walk turns along the river in front of the Royal Naval College near the Trafalgar Tavern. The visit to Greenwich Park includes a flower garden, a deer park, the Royal Observatory, with a marker for the Prime Meridian line, and a panoramic view over London. Finally, the walk goes through Greenwich market with its craft stalls and street food and finishes at Cutty Sark DLR Station, which provides an easy link back to Canary Wharf.

1. From platform level follow the signs for Crossrail Place (not Canada Place). Go up two flights of escalators and leave the station at quayside level (Level-1). Walk ahead across Adams Plaza and take the steps up to the road. Cross at the lights and turn left. After 20m take the ramp or steps on your right to enter Canada Square. Go diagonally across the square and turn right on Upper Bank Street. (In winter you may have to negotiate your way round the ice rink in the centre to reach the far corner.) Just past the entrance to the Jubilee line station, turn right by a red pillar box. Walk through Jubilee Park with its water features and artworks. (*Toilets and refreshments in Jubilee Place Mall.*)

2. Leave the park, going past another entrance to the underground station. Go ahead to the pedestrian lights and cross the road to your left. Walk ahead, slightly to the left, to 35 Bank Street. Go through the foyer of the building and out the other side. Cross the bridge over South Dock. Turn left and walk along the quayside until you reach a water inlet. Turn right by the railings and walk out to a road (Marsh Wall). Cross straight over and go down the steps to the right of South Quay

DLR Station. Walk down the side of Millwall Inner Dock. At a road, turn left and cross Glengall Bridge (a Dutch-style canal bridge). After the bridge, turn right and follow the path around Millwall Outer Dock, with the water on your right. You reach a semi-circular area of grass by an industrial chimney. Go left on the path through its centre and down a flight of steps to go under the DLR. Climb the steps on the other side, cross East Ferry Road and enter Mudchute Park.

3. Climb diagonally up two flights of steps. At the top, turn right and walk along a concrete path. Go through a kissing gate by a green arrow. 150m later, where the path goes left, take a smaller path downhill to the right. Go through a metal gate at the end and turn immediately left into Millwall Park. Turn right and walk around the perimeter of the park, passing the brick arches of an old railway viaduct. Pass to the right of Island Gardens DLR Station, cross a road and continue in the same direction along Douglas Path to reach Greenwich Foot Tunnel. After admiring the view across the Thames to Maritime Greenwich, go through the tunnel. (*The lifts at either end are very often out of order, so be*

The view from Greenwich Park

prepared to walk down 84 steps and up 100 steps on the far side.) You emerge beside the *Cutty Sark*, a 19th century tea clipper. Turn left on the Thames Path, outside the railings to the left of the Visitor Centre and the Royal Naval College, now home to Greenwich University, with views of Canary Wharf and the O2.

4. Halfway along the railings, you reach the ornate wrought iron Water Gate. Go up the steps and through the gate, with views of the Queen's House and the Royal Observatory on the hill ahead, framed by the twin domes of the College. You come to a broad crossing drive, with the Chapel to the left and the Painted Hall to your right, (*both open to visitors*). To continue the walk, turn left along the driveway to the side exit and turn right into Park Row. (*If the Water Gate is closed, continue along the Thames to the Trafalgar Tavern, turn right on Park Row and enter the Naval College through the side gate. After having a good look round, return to Park Row.*) Walk up Park Row and cross the main road at the lights. Continue ahead into Greenwich Park and walk in the same direction slightly uphill. At a five-way junction, take the third exit: a broad tree-lined avenue to the right of a small hill, past a row of benches. The road climbs gently, then more steeply. At the top, by an information board, continue ahead in the same direction across the grass between the trees. When you reach a tarmac path, turn left towards a park exit. Just before the exit, turn right, following signs for *Flower Garden* and *Deer Enclosure*.

5. Enter the Flower Garden through a gate and walk ahead on the broad left-hand path. You soon come to two unsurfaced paths going left. Take the first of these to reach the deer park viewing area. (*At the time of writing, the deer park was being restored and the deer relocated to Richmond Park until 2024.*) Retrace your steps to the main path and turn left to continue through the Flower Garden. At a T-junction, turn right then left to reach a small lake. Keep on ahead past the lake to another T-junction and turn left past a lake viewpoint. The broad path swings left and right to reach the gate which leads to the Flower Garden exit gate. Turn right onto the main park avenue and cross towards

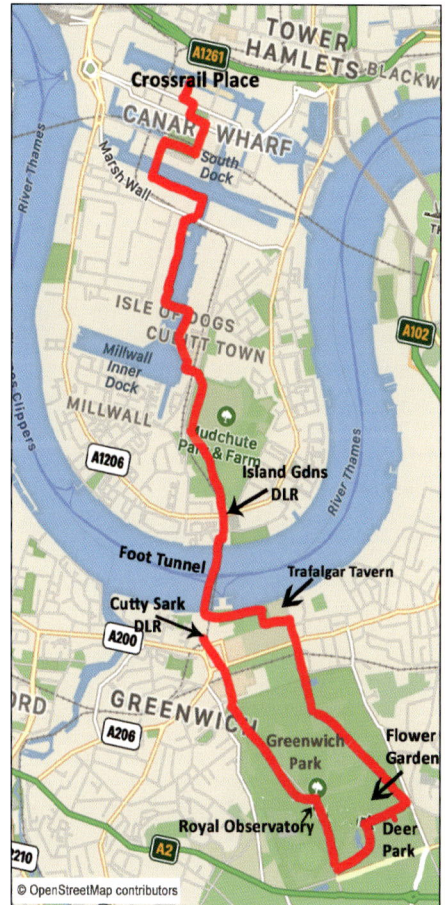

the toilets. To your left there is a good view towards the spire of Blackheath church. Turn right along the tree-lined avenue. Go across a junction and past the Pavilion Café.

6. As you reach the Royal Observatory, one of the best viewpoints in London opens up ahead. To your left are two paths. Just behind a metal gate on the upper path is a marker where you can stand across the Prime Meridian. To continue the walk, take the lower path steeply downhill. At a semi-circular raised area, take the broad path going down to the right. Half-way down, at a circular crossing, go diagonally left down to the main park gates and leave the park. Go ahead on King William Walk, passing the National Maritime Museum. Cross the main road at the lights. Go left then right, still on King William Walk. Cross over and enter Greenwich Market through a passageway. Go down the centre of the market and exit at the far end. Cross to the other side of the road, watching out for traffic from your left, and turn left. Cutty Sark DLR Station is straight ahead, across a side road. Take a train to West India Quay DLR Station, which is next to Crossrail Place and the Canary Wharf Elizabeth line station.

Maritime Greenwich is a World Heritage Site and home not only to the Prime Meridian but also to buildings and museums representing the outstanding achievements of the 17th and 18th centuries in science and architecture. Thanks to its World Heritage status, as well as its links with British monarchs, Greenwich became a Royal Borough in 2012, the year of the London Olympics, when the park was the superb backdrop for 19 days of Olympic and Paralympic equestrian events.

The *Cutty Sark*, built on the Clyde in 1869, is the world's sole surviving tea clipper. She was one of the fastest of her time on trade routes from China, India and Australia. On her maiden voyage to Shanghai she brought back a cargo of tea worth £1.3 million. A fire in 2007 damaged the ship but luckily the masts and other items had been removed for restoration so 90% of the ship was saved.

Greenwich Park is London's oldest Royal Park, dating from 1493. Henry VIII, who was born in Greenwich, introduced deer into the park. James I gave the park to his wife, Queen Anne, who then commissioned Inigo Jones to design the Queen's House. Charles II commissioned Christopher Wren to build the Royal Observatory, now part of the National Maritime Museum. The magnificent cedars and seasonal flower beds set in green lawns make the Flower Garden a favourite spot with visitors of all ages. Overlooking the panoramic view outside the Observatory is a statue of General Wolfe.

Crossrail Place in Canary Wharf is a striking five-storey building with the Elizabeth line platforms on Level -4. A roof garden on Level 1 (the top floor) features plants from the Eastern and Western Hemispheres. The garden has a unique timber lattice roof that lets in light and rain to promote natural growth.

Wanstead Park

8 Manor Park Circular via Wanstead Park and Alexandra Lake

Distance	8 km (5 miles)
Underfoot	Mostly earth paths, some mud after rain
Start	Manor Park Station (Elizabeth line)
Finish	Manor Park Station
Points of Interest	Wanstead Park; Alexandra Lake; Wanstead Flats; City of London Cemetery
Refreshments	Tea Hut (halfway point); Golden Fleece pub and City of London Cemetery café (off route at the end of the walk)
Toilets	Wanstead Park
Shortening the Walk	Omit Wanstead Park, but not recommended as you would miss a delightful part of the walk

Manor Park was once a staging-post on the old Roman road from Aldgate to Colchester, but is now a pleasant suburban area in the London Borough of Newham. This figure-of-eight walk offers a green and pleasant meander along the borders of Epping Forest. There are many waterside sections, including part of the Roding Valley Way, and several ponds and waterways within Wanstead Park, ending with a walk round Alexandra Lake. The Tea Hut in the park, by Heronry Pond, offers welcome refreshments and there is a pub and a café close to the end of the walk. The route skirts the perimeter of one of the largest municipal cemeteries in Europe, the Grade I-listed City of London Cemetery, established in 1826 and covering 200 acres. The footballer Bobby Moore is buried here.

1. Cross the road at the pedestrian crossing outside Manor Park Station and turn left. Cross Forest View Road and enter Manor Park by a *Welcome to Epping Forest* sign. Immediately turn right on a small earth path which runs parallel to Forest View Road. Follow this to the end of the park and arrive at Aldersbrook Road, beside the City of London Cemetery. (*Later in the walk you have the option of visiting this Grade I listed cemetery.*) Cross over and turn right past a set of tall metal gates to enter a narrow alleyway which runs alongside the cemetery wall. The alleyway turns left by a sign for the *Roding Valley Way* and becomes a pleasant tree-lined path between the railway line and the cemetery.

2. Continue for 500m with views of the cemetery through the railings. Reach a crossing track and turn left on the Roding Valley Way. Walk for 1km. The cemetery fence is on your left and there is a small stream and then allotments on your right. At a fork by a signpost, go right following the sign for the *Roding Valley Way*, with the River Roding now visible on your right. Continue ahead along this well-defined path, ignoring any other paths to the left and right, until you reach a T-junction with a broad tarmac track. Turn left here, following a sign for *Wanstead Park*, but then almost immediately turn right onto an unmarked earth path. After passing through some trees you reach a woodland track in front of a stretch of water with a four-way wooden fingerpost. Turn left here along the track, following the signs for *Ornamental Water Walk, Tea Hut* and *The Temple*. Follow the track

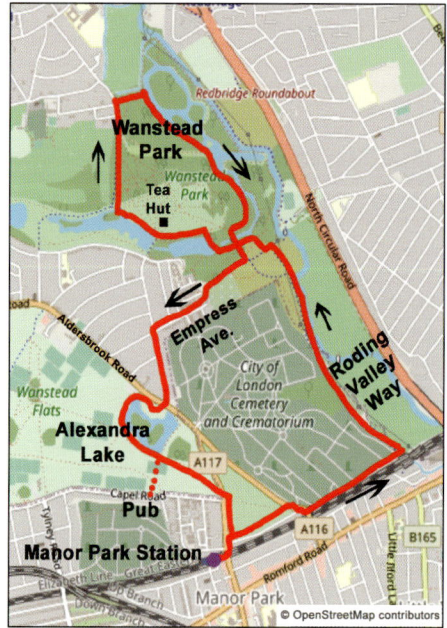

until you reach a small lake, Perch Pond.

3. Turn right, with the pond on your left. At the next corner turn left and continue to walk beside the water. At the far end of the lake you reach a wooden fingerpost just before another pond, Heronry Pond. Just to the right of the fingerpost is the Tea Hut and a picnic area, both highly recommended for a break. (*There are also toilets, 200m past the Tea Hut, part of the building known as The Temple.*) From the fingerpost, take the path signed *Blake Hall Road*, to walk along the right-hand bank of Heronry Pond, in the same direction as before, with the water on your left. At the first corner, turn left by a sign for *Wanstead Park* and *Epping Forest*. Almost immediately turn right to follow a wide path between wooden fences, signposted for *Wanstead Station*. Continue for

300m, then go through some white gates which lead into Warren Road. Continue ahead along Warren Road, passing two residential roads on your left. Shortly after the second road, Warren Drive, take a track on your right which leads back into the woods, by another sign for *Epping Forest*.

4. Walk ahead to a T-junction and turn right on the *Ornamental Water Walk*. After about 300m, go past a fingerpost and then turn left onto a sometimes muddy path towards the remains of a folly visible ahead. This is a Grade II-listed building known as the Grotto. It was partially destroyed by fire in 1884. At the time of writing restoration work on the boat landing stage had been started. Continue to follow the path past the Grotto as it swings right into the woods. At a crossing path with a fingerpost you reach Dell Bridge. Turn left over the bridge and follow the sign for *Ilford via Quiet Way*.

5. Just after the bridge go straight ahead at a junction of woodland tracks. 75m later, leave the woods

and turn right onto a tarmac track. Follow this past a metal barrier as it becomes a lane, passing stables and allotments. Stay on the lane as it swings left and right and emerges at the end of Empress Avenue. Walk along the avenue for 300m to reach a crossroads. Go left into Wanstead Park Avenue and continue to the junction with Aldersbrook Road. (An *optional detour to the left here takes you to the City of London Cemetery, 180m along Aldersbrook Road, with a café and public toilets.*)

6. To continue on the walk, cross Aldersbrook Road at the pedestrian crossing and take a short cut straight ahead from the crossing to join a path which you follow to the right. The path divides into three. All three lead to the Alexandra Lake, but take the path to the left, which then swings right to take you right up to the water's edge. Go right, then left past the car park, then left again to walk the full length of the lake. At the top, the lakeside path goes left, back towards the road. You however continue straight ahead. You come to a wooden marker post where you

Heronry Pond

can turn right on a grassy path to reach the Golden Fleece pub, clearly visible a short distance away on Capel Road. To continue directly to Manor Park Station, go straight ahead at the marker on a path across the grassland of the Wanstead Flats. When you reach the corner where Capel Road meets Forest Drive, cross straight over Forest Drive at the pedestrian crossing and enter Manor Park. Immediately turn right and walk along the inside edge of the park back to Manor Park Station.

Alexandra Lake

The River Roding rises at Molehill Green in Essex and flows for 50 kilometres (30 miles) before joining the Thames at Barking, where it becomes a tidal creek, known as Barking Creek. Epping Forest lies on a ridge between the valleys of the rivers Roding and Lea.

Wanstead Park covers an area of 57 hectares (140 acres) in the London Borough of Redbridge. The park was created by enclosing part of Epping Forest in the mid-16th century. It was once the landscaped park of the magnificent Wanstead House, sadly demolished in the 1820s. The Temple was built in the Tuscan style in the second half of the 18th century by the Earl of Tylney and is one of the few buildings that remain of this once great estate, although its purpose is not entirely clear. At one stage it had become an aviary for exotic birds. The Earl also commissioned the Grotto, a Grade II-listed building. Both Wanstead Park and Wanstead Flats are now managed by the City of London Corporation.

Wanstead Flats, the southernmost part of Epping Forest, is mainly an area of open grassland which was used for cattle grazing until 1996, when BSE brought an end to the custom. The area is prone to both flooding and extreme drying out and the ponds and lakes in the flats are often dry. Alexandra Lake was created in 1907 as part of an unemployment relief scheme. Due to its population of nesting skylarks, the Wanstead Flats is a Site of Special Scientific Interest. The area is also popular with footballers, horse riders, joggers, cyclists, dog walkers, model flying clubs and families.

River Loddon from Whistley Bridge

9 Twyford Circular via Whistley Bridge and the Loddon Valley

Distance	**8 km (5 miles)**
Underfoot	**Countryside and riverside paths, which can be very muddy; Roads at start and finish**
Start	**Twyford Station (Elizabeth line)**
Finish	**Twyford Station**
Points of Interest	**Twyford Village; Whistley Bridge; Loddon Valley Lakes**
Refreshments	**Cafés and pubs in Twyford**
Toilets	**Twyford Station**
Shortening the Walk	**No options**

Twyford is a large village 9.5 km (6 miles) east of Reading. Its name is derived from the Anglo-Saxon for two fords, emphasising its importance as a crossing point of the River Loddon at the place where the river splits into two channels. It was a staging point used by wool merchants for taking their cloth to London. The railway arrived in 1839 and Twyford became a junction between the main line to the West Country and the branch line for Henley. The rail links have made it popular with commuters who work in Reading, Wokingham or London. This picturesque walk goes to the east and south of Twyford and finishes in the village centre. It explores the surrounding countryside using byways, footpaths and tracks, passing the lakes and watercourses of the River Loddon flood plain. At the end of the walk there are several opportunities for refreshments in the village. In winter or after rain this walk will be very muddy. Wellington boots recommended!

1. Come out of Twyford Station and turn right on Station Road. At the end, turn left, past the Golden Cross pub, into Waltham Road. Cross over at the pedestrian traffic lights and turn right into Springfield Park. With a grassy area ahead, go left, then left again to follow Springfield Park out to its junction with a main road (London Road). Turn right and immediately take a right fork into Ruscombe Road signposted *Windsor* and *Waltham St Lawrence*. Follow Ruscombe Road for the next 700m as it swings to the right. Go straight across a junction with New Road and Stanlake Road and 100m further on, where the main road swings left, continue ahead into Southbury Lane towards the church of St James the Great.

2. Go to the right of the church and follow Southbury Lane as it swings right by some houses over a railway bridge. Continue on the lane as it curves round to the right, with a large house over on the right. Where the

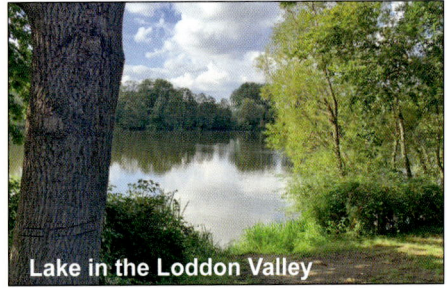
Lake in the Loddon Valley

lane begins to swing back to the left, look out for a signed footpath on the right opposite a house and a thatched cottage. The footpath leads into a large field. Go straight across the field, then go through a metal gate and across a footbridge. Continue ahead in the same direction along a narrow path between a hedge and a fence and follow it out to a road (Waltham Road). Turn left, cross the road and just before a small bridge turn right down some steps onto a footpath with a small stream on your left. Go left at a T-junction of paths and follow this firm path for 500m with a modern housing estate to the right, passing a children's playground on the left. When you come to a road (Broad Hinton), turn left and walk up to the main road (Hurst Road).

3. Turn left for 100m along the footway to where a track comes in from the left. Turn right here to cross the road and enter a track on the opposite side. After 200m, the track drops into a hollow which may be impassable in winter or after rain. To avoid this, turn right on a diversion loop that brings you back to the track 100m further on. Continue in the same direction as before to meet

Loddon Nature Reserve

Whistley Mill Lane. Turn right and go across a bridge where you get a first view of the lakes in this area. Shortly after the bridge, a short stretch of footpath runs parallel to the road on the right by a green footpath sign. If traffic is light you may wish to stay on the road. Further on, take a longer section of off-road path signposted to the left, which provides glimpses of the lake you saw from the bridge.

4. When you meet the road again there is a metal gate on your right. Just after this gate, turn right on a broad footpath. Go ahead for 700m, passing a lake on the left. Go under a railway bridge and turn right beside another lake. You are now in the Loddon Nature Reserve. Walk for 180m and turn left at the corner of the lake. Follow a sign pointing right along a narrow path that soon turns left beside the River Loddon. Follow this path to a bridge. Cross over and pass a residential development. Cross another bridge to reach Weavers Way and make your way out to Old Bath Road on the outskirts of Twyford. Turn right along the road and walk into the village centre, passing the Duke of Wellington pub on your right. Arrive at a crossroads with traffic lights and a coffee shop. Turn right into Church Road and then take a fork into Station Road to reach Twyford Station.

The River Loddon is a tributary of the River Thames. It rises near Basingstoke in Hampshire and flows northwards for 45 km (28 miles) to meet the Thames at Wargrave in Berkshire. The river once had a number of mills with various weirs and sluices used to generate the water power for their operation. One was a silk mill and another a paper mill, with others milling corn to produce flour. Some of these have since been converted to become homes or hotels. Over time, former gravel workings have become lakes and offer diverse habitats for wildlife. The area near Twyford boasts its own flowering bulb: the Loddon Lily, *Leucojum aestivum,* or Summer Snowflake, which has been chosen as Berkshire's county flower. In recent years improvements have been made to the river which include the installation of a fish bypass at Arborfield Mill for migratory species such as salmon.

Tobacco Dock

10 Farringdon to Whitechapel via the South Bank of the Thames and Spirit Quay

Distance	**8.5 km (5 miles)**
Underfoot	**Paved surfaces throughout**
Start	**Farringdon Station (Elizabeth line; London Underground; Thameslink)**
Finish	**Whitechapel Station (Elizabeth line; London Underground)**
Points of Interest	**Smithfield Market; St Bartholomew's; Postman's Park; St Paul's; Millennium Bridge; Southwark Cathedral; Tower Bridge; St Katharine Docks; Tate Modern**
Refreshments	**Many opportunities en route**
Toilets	**Farringdon Station Thameslink Platform 4; Barts Hospital; Paternoster Square; London Bridge Station**
Shortening the Walk	**Finish at London Bridge Station**

This walk takes you from the Victorian splendour of Smithfield Market to the everyday bustle of an East End market. Along the route there are churches, bridges, docks, an unusual memorial, two cathedrals and an art gallery. From Farringdon you make your way through Smithfield Market, past the magnificent churches of St Bartholomew the Great and St Paul's Cathedral, then down to the Millennium Bridge to cross the Thames. You follow the South Bank of the Thames past Southwark Cathedral and cross back over the river at Tower Bridge to visit St Katharine Docks. There follows a stretch along peaceful Spirit Quay before you make your way to Whitechapel Station via Watney Market.

1. Turn right out of Farringdon Station and walk up Cowcross Street. At the end of the street, cross straight over at the traffic lights and go through the grand archway into Smithfield Market and walk along Grand Avenue. Leave the market, cross at the lights and walk ahead on West Smithfield. Go past the entrance to a narrow lane, Cloth Fair, and 20m later reach the half-timbered Tudor gatehouse of St Bartholomew the Great. After taking time to visit this magnificent church, continue in the same direction as before, on Little Britain. (*After 30m, by a large red column on the right, there are toilets and café open to the public just inside the entrance to Barts Hospital.*) Stay on the right-hand side of Little Britain as it turns right at a T-junction. Where Little Britain goes off to the left, continue ahead for a few steps, before crossing over to the left-hand side of King Edward Street at the pedestrian lights. Turn right. St Paul's Cathedral is now visible ahead. At the end of the first building, you reach the entrance to Postman's Park, under a large plane tree. Enter the park and

walk towards St Botolph's church. Before reaching it, go left to visit the Memorial to Heroic Self-Sacrifice, a unique and poignant commemoration of men, women and children who lost their lives while trying to save others.

2. Leave the park by the church and turn right into St Martin Le Grand. 200m later you reach a wide junction, with St Paul's Underground station and a modern octagonal building on the opposite side. Cross at the lights and go behind the station, to the right of the octagonal building, into Panyer Alley. Take the first right, Paternoster Row, to reach Paternoster Square. Walk through the square and leave through a large stone archway on the left, just past the public toilets in Paternoster Lodge. Turn right, staying on the right-hand footway to reach a set of traffic lights. Cross at the lights and turn left, with the cathedral to your left on the opposite side of the road. Just before a small municipal garden, turn right past the entrance to the City of London Information Centre and descend Peter's Hill. Keep straight

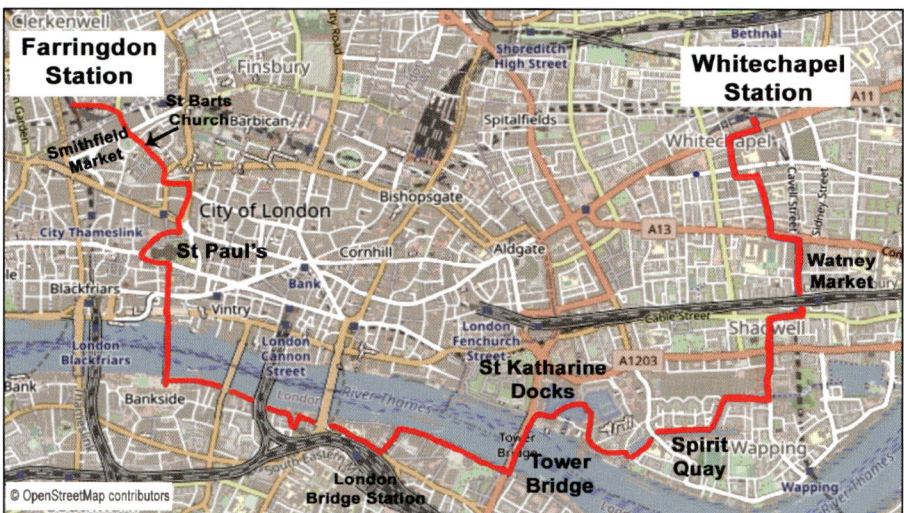

on over the Millennium Bridge with the Tate Modern Art Gallery ahead of you. As you cross the bridge, look behind you for an iconic view of St Paul's.

3. On the other side of the Thames, turn right at the bottom of the ramp to walk along Bankside, with the river on your left, passing Bankside Pier and the Globe Theatre. Go under Southwark Bridge and continue past the Anchor pub. Go right and then left to enter Clink Street, past the Clink Prison Museum and the ruins of the 13th century Bishop's Palace. At the end, pass the full-size replica of the *Golden Hinde*, the boat in which Sir Francis Drake sailed round the world. Swing to the right and arrive at Southwark Cathedral. You may wish to make a short detour here to the right to visit the cathedral and Borough Market. Your onward route, however, goes left behind the cathedral on a brick-surfaced road. Follow the road as it turns right and passes under one of the stone arches of London Bridge. Continue ahead on Tooley Street.

4. You reach a junction opposite an entrance to London Bridge Station. Swing to the left, still on Tooley Street, and after 150m turn left into Hayes Galleria, opposite another entrance to London Bridge Station. *(Public toilets inside the station.)* Go through the Galleria to reach the Thames. Turn right and walk past HMS *Belfast* towards Tower Bridge. Go under the bridge and turn right up some steps to reach the right-hand footway of the bridge, initially following a blue line celebrating those who constructed the bridge. Cross the river and swing right down the steps at the end of the bridge. Turn sharp left at the bottom

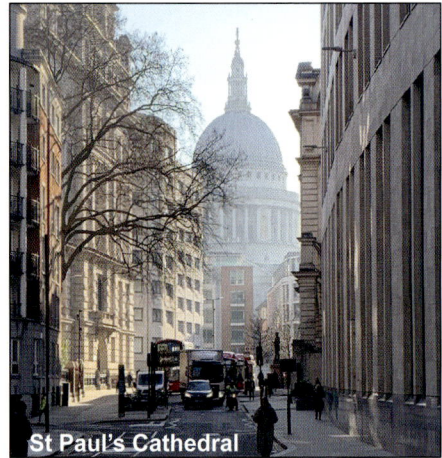
St Paul's Cathedral

and then immediately right by a grey and orange pillar signed *St Katharine Docks*. Go ahead beside the water and turn left after 50m, following the line of the dock past a rotunda Go right across a footbridge. Continue with the water on the right. Go right at the next footbridge towards the Dickens Inn. Walk across a paved open area in front of the inn and leave St Katharine Docks to the left, opposite a red phone box and pillar box. Pass a metal road barrier, swing right and then left onto St Katharine's Way, signposted *Wapping Woods*.

5. At the end of St Katharine's Way, just past Tower Bridge Wharf, turn right onto Wapping High Street. Take the first left, opposite a memorial garden. Just past the sign for *Redmead Lane*, take the path to the left between two pillars and walk along the side of Hermitage Basin. At the end of the basin turn left and then right to descend a long flight of steps, signed *King Edward Memorial Park*. Go under a road bridge to reach Spirit Quay, past a sign for *Shadwell Basin*. Continue on the quayside path along this attractive waterway for 500m as it turns left and then right. When you reach Tobacco Dock, with two large ships in dry dock, climb the steps to reach Wapping Lane, turn left and walk for 200m to a T-junction.

6. Cross at the lights and go ahead on a path through St George's Gardens, with the church on your left. Leave the gardens by a mural of the Battle of Cable Street and turn right on Cable Street. Just after passing Shadwell Overground station, turn left into Watney Street and continue ahead through Watney Market. At the end of the market area, turn left onto Commercial Road. Take the second right, Philpot Street, and go over the first crossing. After crossing Varden Street continue on the pedestrianised part of Philpot Street. After passing Ashfield Street, turn left into Newark Street by the modern buildings of the Royal London Hospital, towards a red brick church, now a Medical Library. Take the first right, Turner Street, and continue to its end, where it meets Whitechapel Road. Turn right and after 170m, cross at the lights to reach Whitechapel Station.

Tower Bridge

St Bartholomew the Great is a priory church built in the Romanesque style in the 12th century. It survived the Great Fire of 1666 and the bombs of both World Wars. The church is considered to have the finest Norman church interior in London.

Postman's Park, named for its popularity with post office workers, is home to the Memorial to Heroic Self-Sacrifice, a collection of 54 wall plaques dedicated to those who gave their life to save others. Created by G. F. Watts, it opened in 1900. Many of those remembered here were children, like 8-year-old Henry James Bristow, who in 1890 saved his little sister from a fire, but died himself from burns and shock.

Tate Modern is housed in the former Bankside Power Station designed by Sir Giles Gilbert Scott and built in two phases in 1947 and 1963. Closed in 1981, it was saved from demolition when it was acquired by the Tate Gallery to house its collection of modern art. Opened in May 2000, it is now one of the most visited free attractions in London.

Tower Bridge, completed in 1894, is one of the newest of the Thames bridges in London, and arguably the most iconic. It is a double-leaf bascule bridge which opens to allow tall ships to pass. In December 1952, a No. 78 bus was crossing the bridge when the driver, Albert Gunter, realised that it was opening. Gunter put his foot down and jumped the bus over the gap, getting all 20 passengers safely across.

Perivale Park

11 Ealing Broadway to Hanwell via the Brent River Walk and Perivale Park

Distance	9 km (5.5 miles)
Underfoot	Paved surfaces; gravel paths
Start	Ealing Broadway Station (Elizabeth line; London Underground)
Finish	Hanwell (Elizabeth line)
Points of Interest	Pitshanger Park; Perivale Park; Brent River Park Walk
Refreshments	Cafés in Pitshanger Park; Perivale Park; Hanwell Zoo
Toilets	Ealing Broadway Station; Pitshanger Park; Perivale Park
Shortening the Walk	Bus from Greenford back to Ealing Broadway

Until the urban expansion of London in the late 19th century, Ealing was a rural village in Middlesex. The opening of the railway in 1838 promoted the local economy of market gardening and led to suburban development. In 1902, Ealing was referred to as *'Queen of Suburbs'* because of its excellent rail connections and its proximity to countryside, with pleasant parks and walks and cycle rides on its doorstep. This walk demonstrates the truth of that judgement. The route goes through several parks and waterside meadows as well as Brentham Garden Suburb as it follows the elusive River Brent to Hanwell. Interesting sights include a maze, a small zoo and a former church with a weatherboarded tower. The widening of the A40 meant the church became separated from its congregation and it has now become a cultural and concert venue.

1. Turn right out of the station and continue until you reach a roundabout. Turn right and go over the road at the zebra crossing. Go ahead, just to the right of the crossing, into Mountfield Road. Go straight ahead at the crossroads with Woodville Road into Hillcroft Crescent. When the road goes left, continue straight ahead on West Walk, a pedestrian and cycle path. Where the path ends, continue along West Road. Follow the road round to the right, in front of a low fence and a recreation ground. After 100m, opposite a water tower, turn left into Fox Lane and walk through Fox Wood Nature Reserve. Continue ahead to a road, where you turn left. At a T-junction go right into Lynwood Road. Go ahead at the junction with Brunswick Road. Just before a dual carriageway (the A40), turn left by a speed limit sign into an unmarked drive between houses and garages.

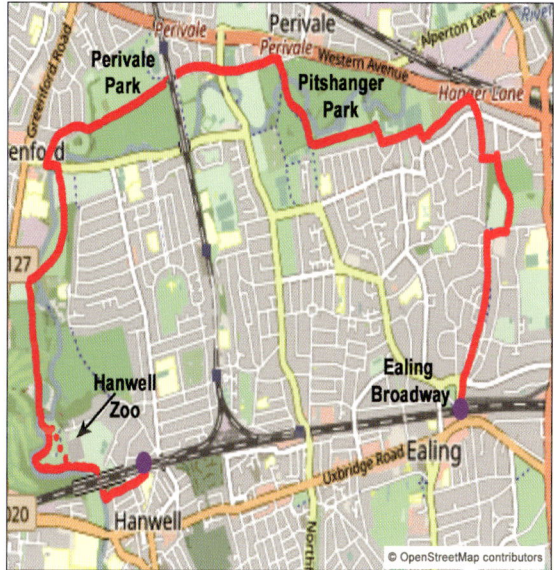

2. Continue on a path with allotments on your right. When you reach a large fence, turn left to reach Brunswick Road. Turn right, following a sign for *Brent River Park Walk*. Take the next right into Neville Road and then the first left into Meadvale Road, which takes you through Brentham Garden Suburb. After 500m, you will see the entrance to Pitshanger Park on your right, opposite Barnfield Road, by a *Brent River Park Walk* sign. Enter the park and keep left on a broad path past the tennis courts. At the far end of the courts, turn right by a café and toilets. Turn left at a crossing path, with a golf course now on your right. Take the next path to the right, signed

for *Perivale*, and continue on this path between fences to go over a large bridge. This is your first sight of the River Brent. Continue past the former church of Saint Mary's with its white weatherboarded tower. (*The old graveyard is a pleasant place for a short break.*) Go through a lychgate and turn left into Perivale Lane, passing behind the Myllet Arms pub on your right. Ignore a cyclepath sign to the right and go ahead, following the sign for *Perivale Station*.

3. Continue up to the junction with Argyle Road. Cross with care at the lights, which do not have a pedestrian phase, and enter the road opposite, Stockdove Way. Just before a railway bridge, ignore the cycle path signs to left and right and go ahead under the bridge towards the Perivale Park Golf café and WCs. Go to the right through the car park and behind the café and go past a vehicle barrier. Ignore the track ahead past the athletics centre. Instead take the gravel path which

River Brent

then immediately right to continue in the same direction as before. (*If it is dry underfoot, you can choose at this point to walk for a short stretch along the riverbank: where the above path goes left, turn right down steps onto a path and go left. This path returns you to the firmer path later on, where you turn right.*) At a T-junction of paths, go right over a wooden bridge to the other bank of the river. Go ahead for 50m and then turn left on a path across a golf course. Walk for 800m until you reach a metal footbridge.

5. After crossing the bridge, there are various routes across the grassy area ahead. You can turn right and follow the *Capital Ring* as it follows the river. Alternatively, you can go up across a grassy slope, walk ahead and descend past the right-hand side of the Millennium Maze, then swing left to rejoin the Capital Ring shortly before a signpost on a raised bank. The third way (recommended) is to go up the grassy bank and swing left towards a playground. Turn left along the side of the playground to the entrance to Hanwell Zoo. Turn right past the café and toilets and left by the entrance to the maze, following the perimeter of the zoo. At the end of the railings, you pass the sign on a raised bank where the Capital Ring comes in from your right. Continue ahead here for 250m. Ignore a path to the left signposted *Hanwell Station* and turn right to go under the railway viaduct (signpost for *Osterley Lock)*. Immediately turn left on a small path going uphill with the viaduct on your left. Turn left again to walk above a small park and continue till you reach Station Road. Cross over, turn right and then left into Station Approach and walk for 150m to reach Hanwell Station.

goes diagonally left. Continue on the firm path, down the line of trees, with playing fields on the right and the golf course to the left. Join a tarmac path coming in from the right and continue ahead. Where a second path comes in, continue ahead across a bridge.

4. Come out into Costons Lane and turn left. You are now on the Capital Ring, which you follow for the rest of the walk. The road swings right to reach a larger road (Ruislip Road) on the outskirts of Greenford. Following the *Capital Ring* signs, turn left on the road bridge over the river, cross to the right-hand side at the zebra crossing and take the signed footpath to the right of the crossing to walk alongside the Brent, which is mostly hidden by trees and undergrowth. After 650m, follow this path as it goes first left

Tylers Common

12 Brentwood to Harold Wood via Tylers Common

Distance	**9 km (5.5 miles)**
Underfoot	**Country paths, muddy in winter and after rain; roads**
Start	**Brentwood Station (Elizabeth line)**
Finish	**Harold Wood Station (Elizabeth line)**
Points of Interest	**Donkey Lane Plantation; Tylers Common**
Refreshments	**Cafés in Warley and Upminster Garden Centre; Café, bakery and supermarket opposite Harold Wood Station**
Toilets	**Brentwood Station; Harold Wood Station**
Shortening the Walk	**Take the No. 496 bus for the final 1.5km**

This walk is an attractive ramble through the countryside that lies just beyond London in Essex. Leaving Brentwood, the walk passes through delightful woodland, carpeted with bluebells in spring. After leaving Headley Common there are some expansive views over the countryside and as you approach the M25, there are distant views towards central London. Once over the motorway, you reach Tylers Common, a large open area of grassland with good views all round. The common supports a wide range of butterflies and the hedgerows are dominated by blackthorn, elm and hawthorn. There is a café at Upminster Garden Centre in Nags Head Lane, towards the end of the walk. In winter or after heavy rain, parts of this walk will be extremely muddy and the walk description includes an alternative route that will keep you away from the worst of this.

1. Leave Brentwood Station via steps up to the Warley Hill exit and turn left over the bridge. Take the first left into Myrtle Road, which soon swings right uphill. After a side road, Myrtle Road becomes Warley Mount. Continue ahead and turn left into Headley Chase at the next junction. Follow Headley Chase as it curves left and right uphill to reach a T-junction with Woodman Road. Turn left and pass the entrance to a cemetery on your right. Take the next road right into Guardsman Close by a footpath sign. Walk to the end of the close and enter the woods. Follow the woodland path ahead. After 180m, there is a four-way junction with a welcome board for *Donkey Lane Plantation*.

2. Cross straight over the junction and continue ahead for another 250m until the path finishes at a wide crossing track. Turn right and continue through a bluebell wood, with a stream over to your left. After 300m, a crossing path comes in from the right. Swing left here and follow this path as it winds between the trees. Shortly after a large clearing, the path continues to the right of a high fence and you come out on a service road for a small industrial estate. Turn right to a larger road (The Drive). Cross over to the opposite footway and turn left to reach a main road. The development on the other side was once the UK headquarters of Ford Motor Company. Turn right and pass a commercial area on your right (*café open until 15.00 and a small local supermarket*). Cross over the main road at the traffic island and turn into Clive

Road. Walk past the Grade II-listed Essex Regiment Chapel, go up to a junction and follow the brown sign for *Brentwood Leisure Park* to the right.

3. Take care along this road, using the verge where possible. Go past the entrance to the leisure park and continue until you reach a smart restaurant and a pond, shortly before a main road (Warley Road). Turn left past the pond onto Headley Common and take the earth path diagonally to the right past a chestnut tree with benches. This brings you up to Warley Road opposite a bus stop. Cross with great care and turn left. Walk 25m to the junction with Great Ropers Lane, where Warley Road swings to the left. Cross over the lane with care and go straight ahead onto a byway with a bridleway and pedestrian sign for a *Quiet Lane*. Continue along the lane, with views to the right, until you reach a T-junction with a small road. Turn left for a few steps and then go right on the path signposted for *Tylers Common*. After 200m, the path swings left and rises between a hedge and a fence to reach a stile with a yellow waymark. Cross the stile and enter a large field. Walk along the left-hand

Footpath to Tylers Common

edge, detouring round a marshy area if necessary. Continue until you reach a metal field gate at the far end. Go through the adjacent kissing gate and follow the path ahead along the edge of a wood, (*with an impressive display of bluebells in early spring*), ignoring smaller paths to the left. Leave the woodland through a kissing gate and cross the pedestrian bridge over the M25. At the far side there are two possible onward routes.

4. Option A: Tylers Common In dry conditions this is the prettier and more direct route, but it is challenging in wet or muddy conditions. Turn left at the end of the bridge and descend to a bend where the path swings left. Leave the main path here and turn right down a couple of steps onto a narrow, uneven footpath into the woods. After 25m you reach a small rickety plank bridge and stile with a red *Private* notice warning you to stay on the footpath. Cross over and enter a large field. Follow the right-hand edge uphill to another stile in the

corner. Cross this stile, ignore a track to the right, and continue up to the left, initially with a hedge to your left. Follow this path as it swings right uphill, ignoring a small path to the left. Just before a junction of paths, you can see a farmhouse to your right. Cross over the wide track that leads to the farm and go ahead for a few steps to a fork. Ahead of you is a line of high-tension cables with a prominent pylon between the two paths. Take the wider path to the left, slightly uphill. (*Wayfinding can be a bit tricky here: your aim in this section is to reach that prominent pylon, which is next to the car park on Nags Head Lane.*) After reaching the top of the hill, the path begins to descend. Go over a crossing path, staying on the broader path as it swings left. At the next junction, cut a corner to swing right downhill. You pass a picnic table and soon reach a road, Nags Head Lane, with a car park (and the pylon) to your right. Cross the lane and enter Harold Court Wood at the signed entrance.

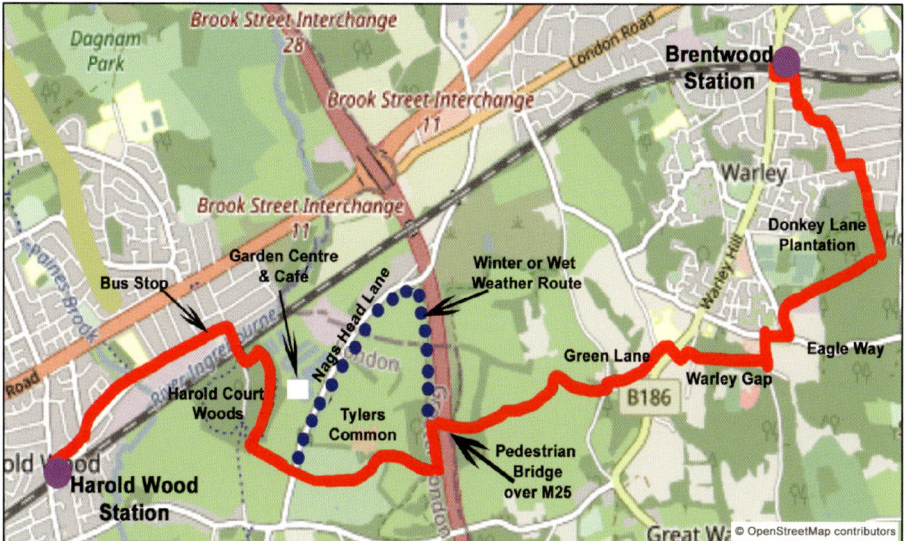

(*For refreshments at the Upminster Garden Centre, turn right for 100m along Nags Head Lane, then return to this point.*)

5. Option B: Nags Head Lane (wet weather or winter) At the end of the motorway bridge go ahead uphill for a few steps and then turn right on a track beside the motorway but at a higher elevation. Continue for 850m as it descends to reach Nags Head Lane. Turn left along the lane, away from the motorway. The path now becomes enclosed with a hedge between you and the lane. If the path is unpleasantly muddy, you can walk along the lane itself. Continue ahead for a further 850m, past the entrance to Upminster Garden Centre, where there is a café. Continue along Nags Head Lane for another 100m, keeping a lookout for the signed entrance to Harold Court Woods on your right, just past a small car park.

6. Both Routes Go through the entrance into Harold Court Woods and turn right. Follow this path for 300m until you reach a junction where a marker post with a white arrow indicates a bridleway to the left. You however, turn right here on the non-bridleway path and follow the arrows which indicate (in very small writing) the way to the car park, passing several benches and a small pond. Where the bridleway comes in from the left, turn right to reach the car park. Go through the car park and turn right under a railway bridge to enter a suburban road that rises up to a junction with Church Street. Turn left here. This marks the end of the scenic part of the route and you now have 1.5km of street walking along Church Road to reach Harold Wood Station. You may prefer to catch the 496 bus, which operates a frequent service from the bus stop on Church Road to Harold Wood Station.

Bluebells on the way to Tylers Common

Little Venice

13 Paddington to St Pancras via Regent's Park and Regent's Canal

Distance	9 km (5.5 miles)
Underfoot	Paved surfaces throughout
Start	Paddington Elizabeth line station
Finish	St Pancras or King's Cross Stations (London Underground; mainline)
Points of Interest	Paddington Basin; Little Venice; Regent's Canal; Regent's Park; Camden Lock; Coal Drops Yard
Refreshments	Paddington Basin; Regent's Park; Camden Lock; Coal Drops Yard
Toilets	Paddington Station; Regent's Park; St Pancras Station
Shortening the Walk	Omit the Regent's Park section by continuing along the canal towpath at Bridge 8

This walk offers plenty of interesting sights. It explores the Regent's Canal between Little Venice and St Pancras and takes in some of the highlights of Regent's Park. The canal towpath provides a pleasant traffic-free route through the capital and is popular with walkers and cyclists. Regent's Park has formal gardens, a boating lake, children's playgrounds, cafés and refreshment stalls. It is also home to London Zoo. Its open green spaces and gardens offer the opportunity for a peaceful break before bustling Camden Lock, the next highlight of the walk. Approaching the end of the walk, you pass through an area of stunning architecture and urban regeneration centred on Coal Drops Yard and Granary Square.

1. Leave Paddington Elizabeth line station and cross into the main concourse of Paddington Station. Go across to the opposite side and follow the signs for *Taxis* and *Hammersmith and City* line, to the right of platform 12, past the station toilets. Take the escalator up to a wide walkway. Continue ahead past the taxi ranks, following signs for the Underground. Just before the entrance to the Underground station, turn right up steps with signs for *Little Venice* and *Paddington Basin*. You come out onto the towpath of the Paddington Arm of the Grand Union Canal. Turn left here on the towpath, going past many cafés, restaurants and moored narrowboats. Go under two bridges. At a third bridge there is a *Welcome to Little Venice* information board.

2. Go under the bridge to arrive in Little Venice at the junction of the Regent's Canal and the Grand Union Canal. Go to the end of the basin, and up a ramp to the right to cross a blue footbridge, with a Jubilee Greenway Marker. The bridge curves down to the right to meet the Regent's Canal. Go ahead on the tow-path as it swings to the left. After going under a bridge, you come to a private section where you take the exit ramp up to the road on your left towards a sign for *Regent's Canal* and *Edgware Road*. Turn right on the footway to reach a main road (the Edgware Road) where the canal goes

into the Maida Hill tunnel. Go briefly to the right by a small restaurant with a conservatory over the canal and cross the road at the lights. Continue ahead into Aberdeen Place, walking in the same direction as before, on the right-hand footway. Where the road turns left, continue straight ahead into an alleyway by a *Greenway* marker and return to the canal, but at a higher level than before.

3. At another main road (Lisson Grove), turn right and cross to the opposite side of the road at the lights. Go ahead through the wrought iron archway signed for *Regent's Canal*. Go down a ramp to walk along the towpath on the right-hand side of the canal. After 300m, follow the towpath across a pedestrian bridge to reach the opposite side of the canal. Go down the ramp at the end and turn left to continue to walk in the same direction as previously. Go under two bridges, passing a row of opulent mansions along the opposite bank in Regent's Park. When you reach the next bridge (Bridge 8) go under it, turn

left and climb the ramp up to street level. (*Should you wish to shorten the walk, do not go over the bridge here but continue on the towpath to reach Camden Lock.*) Cross the bridge and then go over a road to enter Regent's Park. Go right immediately at a fork and keep right at the next fork. When you reach the junction by the Boat Lake Kiosk, turn right past the public toilets and cross two small bridges.

Broad Walk, Regent's Park

4. Turn left and walk down the side of the lake, passing the Boat Lake Café, with the water on your left and a larger bridge visible ahead. When you reach the bridge, cross over the lake and turn left, following a sign for the *Open Air Theatre*. Stay on the path as it swings away from the waterside by the bandstand. Go up to a road, the Inner Circle. Cross straight over and enter Queen Mary's Gardens by a large café. Just past the café, turn left by an *Open Air Theatre* sign and then take the first right. Keep ahead at a crossroads, with the Triton Fountain visible over to your left, and follow a sign to *London Zoo, Camden Town* and *WCs.* Walk past the public toilets towards ornamental gates. Go past the gates, cross the road (the Inner Circle again) and continue ahead into Chester Road. Pass the Allotments Garden on your left and go left into Broad Walk by a zebra crossing. Continue on this pleasant tree-lined avenue for a kilometre, going past a café, the Ready Money drinking fountain and ZSL London Zoo. When you reach a road, cross at the lights and go ahead over a canal bridge.

As you cross the bridge you can see to your right a local landmark: a floating Chinese restaurant in classic red and gold. Turn right along the footway. After 30m go right by a sign for *Regent's Canal Towpath*. Turn left down narrow steps to reach the canal, or take the ramp. Turn left on the towpath. (*This is where the shorter walk comes in.*)

5. Continue for 700m to reach the Camden double locks, whose official name is Hampstead Road Locks, just after a steep humpback section of towpath. To visit the market, go left through an archway by a *Jubilee Greenway* marker (just before a pedestrian bridge). Turn right towards a water inlet, and walk all the way around it, through the maze of street

Camden Market

Regent's Canal by Regent's Park

food stalls, before going left to rejoin the towpath. For a quieter route, with a good view of the activity around the locks, cross over to the other side of the canal via the footbridge. Go past the double lock to reach Camden High Street and turn left over the road bridge, using the right-hand footway. At the end, turn right past a metal gate on a walkway past a row of cafés and go down steps to return to the towpath. Walk on for 1.5km to reach Coal Drops Yard and Granary Square.

6. You pass three former gas holders, now reinvented as luxury apartments. On the other side of the canal, behind the lock-keeper's house, is a relocated water tower (*occasionally open to the public*), which provided water for the steam engines at St Pancras. At this point, leave the towpath and take the path to the left which runs parallel to the towpath at a slightly higher level. This leads you past Coal Drops Yard with its boutiques and restaurants. The path then slopes down to Granary Square, with the buildings of Central St Martins (London University of the Arts) to your left. Take the first bridge on your right (the Esperance Bridge) to cross the canal. Cross over the road and continue ahead into an attractive pedestrian area, Pancras Square. At the end, you reach a brick building, once a gymnasium, now a restaurant. Bear right here for St Pancras Station or left for King's Cross.

Regent's Canal, named after the Prince Regent, later George IV, was built to link the Grand Junction Canal with the Thames. Starting at Little Venice and finishing at Limehouse, it once carried huge quantities of goods through London.

Regent's Park, named after the same Prince Regent, is one of eight royal parks and was developed on a former royal hunting ground. Opened to the public in 1841, highlights include Queen Mary's Rose Garden, the boating lake, the Ready Money drinking fountain, the Triton Fountain and the Jubilee Gates.

Camden Market is well known for its cosmopolitan flair. As well as stalls selling clothing, crafts and bric-a-brac, it has a thriving street food section. The market is one of the most popular visitor attractions in London and draws about a quarter of a million people each week.

Coal Drops Yard was built in 1850 as a coal distribution centre and storage facility. The three-storey sheds were connected to a railway viaduct. Trains came in on the top storey with coal from South Yorkshire. The coal fell down chutes to the hopper floor for sorting before being lowered to boats or road vehicles below. By 2008 the buildings had become derelict, and were being used for illegal raves, but the King's Cross regeneration project has turned them into a shopping and dining hotspot.

Beckton District Park

14 Custom House to Stratford via Beckton Park and the Greenway

Distance	9.5 km (6 miles)
Underfoot	Paved surfaces throughout
Start	Custom House (Elizabeth line; DLR)
Finish	Stratford (Elizabeth line; DLR; Underground; mainline)
Points of Interest	Beckton District Park; The Greenway; The Queen Elizabeth Olympic Park; Westfield Shopping Centre
Refreshments	Olympic Park; Westfield
Toilets	Olympic Park; Westfield
Shortening the Walk	Leave the Greenway at West Ham Station

This walk is a mini-exploration of the London Borough of Newham, which is one of the most populous and ethnically diverse boroughs in London. It crosses the borough from the modest oasis of Cundy Park near Custom House Station to the greater splendours of the Olympic Park at Stratford. Near the start, it visits the pleasant greenery of Beckton District Park with its attractive lake and waterfowl. Next, it follows a 4 km stretch of rooftop-level footpath along the Greenway, which provides a striking panorama of London's skyline stretching as far as the City of London, and a close-up view of Abbey Mills Pumping Station built in the 19th century in a cruciform shape to accommodate the engines within. The Greenway leads directly to the Queen Elizabeth Olympic Park where you will pass close to the ArcelorMittal Orbit Tower, the London Stadium and the Aquatics Centre. The final section leads to Stratford Station via the walkways of Westfield Shopping Centre with its many restaurants and shops.

1. Leave the station via the main exit (Victoria Dock Road). Turn right, away from the ExCel Centre, on a high-level walkway. Go down the steps to street level, swinging right into Freemasons Road. Cross over the road towards the Ibis hotel. Go left, then right into Ethel Road. At the end of the road turn right into an alleyway, just before reaching a small car parking area. Turn left into the next alleyway, which leads into Cundy Park, visible ahead. Go straight ahead in the park for 100m, then take the right fork by three conifers. At the next junction of paths, continue in the same direction with railings and a wall on your left. Leave the park at Prince Regent Lane.

2. Cross over at the zebra crossing towards Royal Docks Academy, and go left. Take the first right into Alnwick Road, following a blue sign for *King George V Park* and continue along the perimeter of the school. When you reach the end of the school fence, look out for a red brick church on your right. When you are on a level with the church, turn left into Baxter Road. Turn right into Randolph Approach by a blue sign. Walk up to a T-junction and turn left by a white sign for the Visitor Centre car park. Go through the car park gates and turn right into King George V Park. Keep right to go past the Visitor Centre. Swing right again at a signpost for *Way Out, King George V Avenue,* going past what was once the Newham City Farm. Leave the park

and turn left. (*If the car park gates are closed, retrace your steps, go past the T-junction, and then turn left into King George V Avenue.*)

3. Where King George V Avenue goes right, keep straight ahead on a path to the left of Calverton School. You reach Stansfeld Road. The large green space ahead behind a low boundary fence is the southern part of Beckton District Park. Turn right here along the road and cross over at the zebra crossing a short distance ahead. Just to the left of the zebra crossing, take the path going diagonally left uphill to enter the park, signposted *Capital Ring*. Follow this path without deviation to where it ends at Tollgate Road. Cross over and enter the northern section of Beckton District Park. Take the path to the left that leads you up the side of the park. Keep left past a café (*closed at the time of writing*) and continue around the lake, passing a rocky promontory. When you arrive at a junction of paths by a red and white

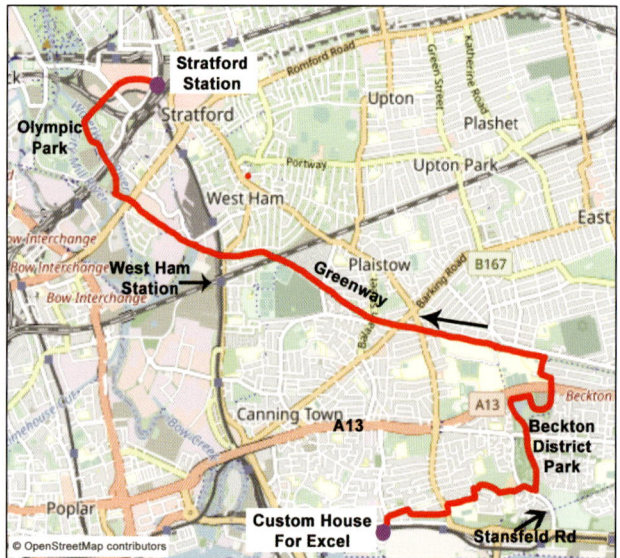

marker, just after passing a small 'beach' area, turn left away from the lake. Swing left where a path comes in from the right and keep left at two more junctions.

4. Go through the gates to leave the park and keep ahead to enter Viking Gardens, ignoring a path to the right. Walk up Viking Gardens to reach the busy A13, which you cross via a pedestrian bridge. On the other side, continue in the same direction up Noel Road, still following the signs for the *Capital Ring*. Turn left into Roman Road, then right into Stokes Road. Ahead, you can see a flight of steps leading up an embankment. Climb the steps and turn left onto the Greenway. After 3 km there is an exit to West Ham Station. The walk continues along the Greenway for another 1.3 km, passing Abbey Mills Pumping Station. You then arrive at a main road (Stratford High Street) with the Olympic Park ahead.

5. Cross at the traffic lights and go ahead across the bridge over the Waterworks River. At the end of the bridge turn right past a multitude of Jubilee Greenway signs embedded in the pavement. Follow the path under a railway and a road bridge, with the Waterworks River hidden to your right until you arrive at the Stratford Waterfront. Stay close to the water

to go under a blue bridge. At a fork, go left up a ramp and then steps towards the ArcelorMittal Orbit. Turn right and continue ahead, with public toilets and a café on your left. 100m later you reach Waterworks Place, with the London Stadium to your left and a bridge to the right. Go over the bridge and walk past the Aquatics Centre. Cross Westfield Avenue at the lights, and continue into Westfield Shopping Centre. Swing right at a fork by a black obelisk and continue on the broad walkway between shops. Just before a very wide pedestrian bridge, look out for an escalator to your left and go down to reach Stratford Station.

The Greenway

The Greenway is a 7 km long footpath and cycleway above the *Joseph Bazalgette Northern Outfall Sewer*, a gravity sewer running from Hackney to Beckton Sewage Treatment Works. It was built after a serious outbreak of cholera in 1853 to improve sanitation in London and is now popular with walkers, cyclists and joggers.

Queen Elizabeth Olympic Park is a legacy of the 2012 London Olympic Games and a popular attraction with its many waterways, wetland areas, flowers and trees. The East Bank is currently being developed as an arts hub and will house a branch of the Victoria & Albert Museum and a University College London campus.

Victoria Park

15 Stratford to Canary Wharf via Victoria Park and the Regent's Canal

Distance	10 km (6 miles)
Underfoot	Paved surfaces throughout
Start	Stratford Station (Elizabeth line; mainline; DLR; London Undergound)
Finish	Canary Wharf Crossrail Place (Elizabeth line) or Canary Wharf (DLR; London Underground)
Points of Interest	Olympic Park; Lee Navigation; Hertford Union Canal; Victoria Park; Regent's Canal; Limehouse Basin
Refreshments	Westfield; Victoria Park; Narrow Street; Canary Wharf
Toilets	Stratford (Westfield); Victoria Park; Canary Wharf
Shortening the Walk	Finish at Limehouse Basin DLR Station

This walk is rarely far from water, with three rivers, two canals and a lake to explore. It starts by taking you through the Queen Elizabeth Olympic Park, past the Aquatics Centre and the London Stadium. After following an arm of the River Lea to reach the Lee Navigation at Old Ford Lock, you go north along the Lee Navigation before leaving it to join the Hertford Union Canal, which leads you to Victoria Park, with its lakes, cafés and open spaces. Leaving the park, you join the towpath of the Regent's Canal and turn south. At the end of the canal you walk around the picturesque Limehouse Basin before passing through a small park called Ropemakers Field. In Narrow Street you can visit a historic pub before following the Thames Path along an attractive section of riverfront to Canary Wharf and the Elizabeth line station at Crossrail Place.

Start of the Walk

slopes down to the City Mill river. With the water on your left, walk towards a blue bridge. Cross over, following a sign for *Old Forde (sic) Lock* and *Hackney Wick*. Continue, now with the Old River Lea on your right and the London Stadium to your left. Shortly after passing under two

1. From the Crossrail platform go down the steps to the underpass, following the signs for *Westfield* and the *Queen Elizabeth Olympic Park*. After the ticket barriers, you pass the entrance to the Westfield Stratford City shopping mall (*toilets inside*). To start the walk, stay outside. Go right towards an *Olympic Park* sign. Turn left up an escalator. At the top, walk slightly to the right along a wide high-level walkway. At a fork, keep left past an obelisk. Cross over Westfield Avenue and continue ahead towards the London Stadium, passing the Aquatics Centre. Cross the wide bridge over the Waterworks River. Just before a second bridge by the London Stadium, turn right on a path that

large black pipes, turn right on a narrow footbridge to Old Ford Lock and the Lee Navigation. Pass to the right of the lock and continue ahead along the towpath for 500m going under two bridges. You will see the entrance to the Hertford Union Canal on the other side of the Lee Navigation.

2. At the third bridge, by the East London Energy centre, which has a distinctive brown flue, go up a ramp, cross the Lee Navigation and turn left down the ramp on the opposite side. Continue ahead on the towpath as it turns right along the Hertford Union Canal, passing

Regent's Canal near Mile End

Bottom and Middle Lock. At the third lock (Top Lock!), pass under a footbridge and then leave the canal by turning right up a ramp. At the top, go left to enter Victoria Park. Turn left and walk along a broad drive above the canal. The park is divided into two sections, each with a café, lake and public toilets. Continue through this first section and just before you reach a road, fork right towards the Jubilee Gate and cross at a zebra crossing. When you enter the next section of the park you arrive at the Pavilion Café, West Lake and toilets.

3. Walk left along the lakeside. The path curves right and you can see to your left the park railings. At this point, with the ornamental pagoda visible ahead in the lake, watch out for a small blue sign for *Cyclepath 1,* which points to the left towards a small gate in the perimeter railings. Turn left here to leave the park and join the towpath of the Regent's Canal by Old Ford lock. Turn left down the canal towpath and walk for 3 km until you reach the end of the canal at Limehouse Basin, where you come to a lock and also a modern footbridge. If you decide to terminate the walk at Limehouse DLR Station, turn right here over the footbridge.

4. To finish at Canary Wharf, only 2 km away, go up to the basin, follow the path along the quayside to the left and go round an inlet passing an information board. After a sign for *Canary Wharf* and *Ropemakers Field,* cross over a metal

bridge. Go down the steps at the end and swing right under the bridge for a short stretch on the Limehouse Cut. Where the cut goes sharp left, follow a sign for the *Thames Path* and *Riverside Pubs* to the right and enter Ropemakers Field. Turn right through the centre of this small park to reach Narrow Street. (*The historic Grapes public house is just over to your right.*) Turn left along Narrow Street for 40m, then turn right by a *Cyclists Dismount* sign through a walkway, next to Dunbar Wharf, to reach the Thames. Go to the left across the curved footbridge and walk along the Thames Path to Canary Wharf pier. Turn left up the broad flight of steps to Westferry Circus. Walk straight ahead through the centre of the Circus, cross over the road and go up the left-hand side of West India Avenue, passing No. 11. Take the first left, signposted *East London Family Court,* to Columbus Courtyard. Go ahead and take the steps to the right at the end to North Dock. Continue on Fisherman's Walk, with the water on your left, to reach Canary Wharf Elizabeth line station.

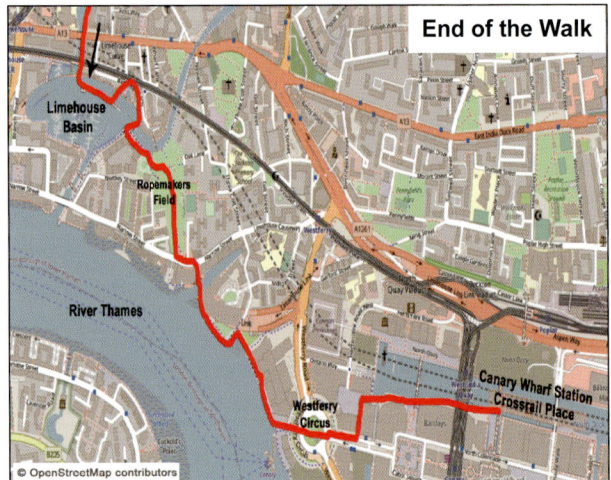

End of the Walk

© OpenStreetMap contributors

Grand Union Canal, Brentford

16 Hanwell to Richmond via the Grand Union Canal, Syon Park and Isleworth

Distance	10 km (6 miles)
Underfoot	Paved surfaces; riverside paths; towpaths
Start	Hanwell Station (Elizabeth line)
Finish	Richmond Station (London Underground; mainline)
Points of Interest	River Brent; Grand Union Canal; Hanwell flight of locks; Syon Park; Isleworth waterfront; the Thames; Richmond
Refreshments	Café in Syon Park Garden Centre; pubs at Hanwell, Brentford, Isleworth and Richmond
Toilets	Hanwell Station; Syon Park; Richmond Station
Shortening the Walk	Bus or train from Brentford

This delightful excursion takes you away from the east-west corridor of Crossrail and leads you to the south bank of the Thames at Richmond. It starts by tracing the River Brent to its junction with the Grand Union Canal and then follows the canal as it makes its way south to Brentford. After passing through the green and tranquil Syon Park you arrive at the attractive waterfront at Isleworth, with two riverside pubs. The walk then joins the Thames Path, which crosses the river at Richmond Lock and follows the river bank to Richmond. At the end of the walk you have the option of exploring the attractions of Richmond town centre. The walk finishes at Richmond Station, from where you can take a fast mainline train to Waterloo, or return to the Elizabeth line by taking the District line via Turnham Green to reach Ealing Broadway.

1. At Hanwell, go down to the underpass, turn right and follow the sign for the Station Approach exit. Turn right again and walk for 150m to reach Station Road. Cross over, go right then left onto a signed footpath beside the railway. At a fork go right by an information board and continue down to a junction next to the Wharncliffe Viaduct. Go straight ahead across a small bridge over the River Brent. Turn left into Brent Meadow with the river on your left. Walk a little further on, then look back at the viaduct, designed by Isambard Kingdom Brunel in 1836. 270m long and 21m high, it carries the Great Western Railway and Elizabeth line over the Brent Valley and was the first major engineering project completed by Brunel. Keep to the left-hand side of the meadow. Just before reaching a busy main road (Uxbridge Road), keep left to a small fork with *Capital Ring* markers pointing to both sides.

2a. Take the main path to the left down to Hanwell Bridge and go under the bridge and up towards a broad path on the other side, where you turn left.

2b. If you find that the path under the bridge is flooded, or simply too muddy to pass, go up the short flight of steps to the right and swing left up to the road. The onward path is straight over on the opposite side, but you should use the traffic lights to your left by the Viaduct pub. Turn right and walk back over the bridge. At the end go left onto a broad path to the right of the river.

3. After 500m on the riverside path, watch out for a substantial brick pillar on your right at the end of a brick wall. Turn right on a cut-through after the pillar to reach the Grand Union Canal by the Hanwell flight of locks. (Don't worry if you miss this turn, as the path you are on soon joins the canal by the last of the locks.) Turn left on the towpath. After crossing a bridge where the River Brent joins the canal, you see a sign for the Fox public house, which is just down to the left. This is not the end of the river. As you carry on down the canal you will see sections which act as overflow and feeder channels. Swing right at one such section over a bridge and follow the left-hand canal towpath for 2km, passing under the M4 motorway and the Piccadilly line.

4. When you reach an arched pedestrian bridge, cross to the other side of the canal and walk along the

Richmond Lock

right-hand bank for another 2 km to Brentford, with the impressive GSK building on the opposite side of the canal. After reaching Brentford Lock, the towpath ends at a brightly painted bridge which carries the London Road. Do not cross London Road here, but swing right to cross Commercial Road at the traffic lights and continue along the right-hand side of London Road for 200m to pedestrian lights by a *Capital Ring* sign pointing left. Cross over and continue ahead along Half Moon Close, which leads to Syon Park. Go down a cycle and pedestrian path with high walls on either side and emerge in the park beside a garden centre which offers a café and toilets. After passing the garden centre, you come up to a small road going through the park.

Swing left here on a footpath past Syon House, visible on your left. Continue on this path along the edge of the park with the road to your right. Go past the gates at the end and turn left into Park Road, by a *Thames Path* sign, to reach the River Thames at Isleworth, with attractive views up and down the river.

5. Turn right into Church Street and continue to the right of the London Apprentice public house. Cross over the Duke of Northumberland's River and turn immediately left to return to the Thames. Go to the right along the quayside. The Thames Path goes ahead across the terrace of Town Wharf pub and at Lion Wharf Road continues through a gateway to follow the river. Follow the path as it swings away from

Isleworth Waterfront

the Thames and reaches a road. Turn left and just before a *Welcome to Richmond* notice, take the first left past a *Thames Path* sign to return to the river. Go ahead for 300m to Richmond Lock and climb the steps to cross the bridge. On the other side, turn right on the Thames Path towards Richmond. Go under a road bridge then a rail bridge. Immediately after the railway bridge, turn left into Old Palace Lane, past the White Swan pub, to reach Richmond Green. To go directly to the station, take the path diagonally across the centre of the Green and then turn left along Little Green. Walk past the theatre and library and then turn right down an alleyway on the right, where Little Green becomes Parkshot, by a *Capital Ring* sign, to emerge opposite Richmond Station.

To visit the town centre, do not take the diagonal path across the Green but go to the right parallel to a road. At the end of the Green cross a road towards the Prince's Head pub. Go down an alleyway to the left of the pub that brings you out on the main shopping street. Turn left and follow this street (George Street, then The Quadrant) to the station.

Wharncliffe Viaduct

Richmond Lock is the furthest downstream of the Thames locks. It is operated by the Port of London Authority. In 1832, the demolition of the narrow arches of Old London Bridge meant tides on the upper river rose and fell more than before. The river at Richmond was then often little more than a stream running through mudbanks. The Richmond half-tide lock, with three vertical steel sluice gates suspended from the footbridge, maintains a navigable depth of water upstream of Richmond, allowing river traffic to avoid the lock for two hours either side of high tide.

Syon House is the London home of the Duke of Northumberland. Built at the end of the 16th century on the site of a medieval abbey, it has been lived in by the Percy family since 1594. The house was redesigned by Robert Adam in the classical style in the 1760s and the interiors are considered to be some of his best work. The extensive Grade I-listed gardens and park were created by Capability Brown.

The Grand Union Canal was built as a commercial link between Birmingham and London. The longest canal in the UK, it runs for 220km (137 miles). The canal was originally known as the Grand Junction Canal.

Jubilee River Boardwalk

17 Slough to Taplow via Herschel Park and the Jubilee River

Distance	**11 km (7 miles)**
Underfoot	**Firm surfaces throughout, apart from a short stretch of woodland path near the end**
Start	**Slough Station (Elizabeth line; mainline)**
Finish	**Taplow Station (Elizabeth line)**
Points of Interest	**Herschel Park; Jubilee River; Dorney Wetlands and Boardwalk**
Refreshments	**Cafés in Slough; picnic site by the river at Dorney**
Toilets	**Slough Station; Taplow Station**
Shortening the Walk	**No options**

Slough is a large town in Berkshire, 32 km (20 miles) west of central London. Its population is one of the most ethnically diverse in the United Kingdom, attracting people from across the world since the 1920s, which has helped to shape it into a major trading centre. This is an easy walk that follows a well constructed cycle and walking track along the beautiful but man-made Jubilee River. Constructed for flood relief, there are practically no built-up areas along its length, which gives the river a remote feel. The reed-beds and trees lining the river are an important wildlife habitat. It is a lovely walk in any season, but in winter you will get the best views of the river through the bare branches of the trees. Apart from the 850m woodland path section at the end, you will be on firm surfaces throughout.

1. Leave Slough Station and walk straight ahead past a large Tesco supermarket. When you reach the main road, cross at the lights, or use the elaborate footbridge, towards the shopping mall on the opposite side. Turn right and then, just before the Catholic church, take a pedestrian route to the left that goes down the side of the shopping mall, signposted to *Town Centre*. When you reach the High Street, turn left. At the start of the pedestrian zone, turn right into Church Street.

Herschel Park

2. Cross straight over Herschel Road and go past the church of St Mary and its large burial ground. When you reach a T-junction, turn right, cross over with care, and take the first left into Upton Park, a private road. The Diana Lodge on the corner has a frieze depicting the goddess Diana hunting a stag. Go ahead at a small crossroads and enter Herschel Park through the gates which have a lamppost on either side. Go to the right, but then swing left, towards two small lakes. When you are at the level of a bridge, turn left and then immediately right at a fork in the path, and keep right at the next fork. The path leads out of the park and into the Nature Reserve.

3. The surfaced path veers left by a sign for the car park, but you take the upper unsurfaced path. This path also leads to the car park. When you reach it, swing right on the footpath to go up to Datchet Road. Turn right on a wide shared cycle and pedestrian path and follow the road across a bridge over the M4. At the end of the bridge there is a speed limit sign. Turn sharp right here on a signed tarmac footpath that takes you steeply down to the turning circle at the end of The Myrke, a small

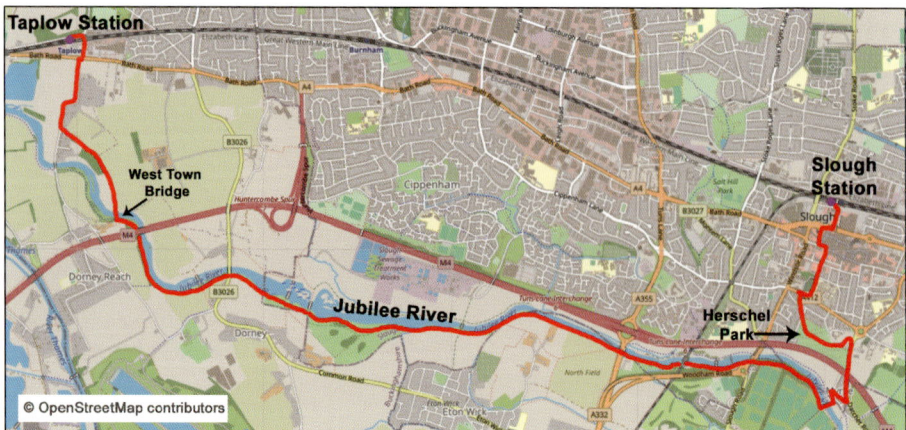

Jubilee River and Weir

residential road. Turn left and after 200m follow the footpath and cyclepath signs to the right, towards a bridge across the Jubilee River. Cross the bridge and turn immediately right at the end, by an Eton College sign. You now follow the Jubilee Riverway and Cyclepath 61 for 7km, staying always close to the river, which is always on your right.

4. As you enter a pleasant wooded section, you have a view over the playing fields of Eton to your left. 800m later you reach Slough Road, which you will have to cross at the traffic lights, with a large roundabout to your left. A fingerpost here shows distances and times to Burnham, Slough and Maidenhead. Go left towards the roundabout but before reaching it, turn right to rejoin the Jubilee Riverway on the same side of the river as before. Go past Slough weir, still following Cyclepath 61 signs. After passing a second weir (Manor Farm weir), there is an open grassy area with picnic tables, close to the Manor Farm bridleway bridge. Just after the bridge, you can take an

interesting detour round a short circular route on a boardwalk in the Dorney Wetlands, which goes right along the water's edge. Access the boardwalk via a wooden pedestrian gate on the right, by an Environment Agency information board.

5. After 6.75 km along the riverside, you go through an underpass under the M4. 180m after that you leave Cyclepath 61 by crossing to the other side of the river via West Town Farm Bridge, Bridge 8, following a footpath sign. Continue ahead for 850m on a pleasant tree-lined path between fields. The first section may be a little muddy. The path ends at Marsh Lane. You now have less than a kilometre to

Jubilee Riverway

walk before reaching Taplow station. (*As an alternative to the footpath, continue ahead on the cyclepath at West Town Farm Bridge and join Marsh Lane by Marsh Lane Weir, adding a couple of hundred metres to the overall distance.*) Turn right on Marsh Lane and follow it to the junction with the A4 (Bath Road). Cross carefully at the traffic island, as the traffic lights here do not have a pedestrian phase. Go ahead, following the sign for the station and Taplow village. Take the access road to the left through the station car park to reach the Bath Road entrance to the station.

Dorney Footbridge

The Jubilee River is a large man-made channel which reduces the risk of flooding in Maidenhead, Windsor and Eton by taking water from the left bank of the Thames upstream of Maidenhead and returning it to the Thames downstream of Eton. It is 12 km long with an average width of 45m and was constructed to look like a natural river. Conception to fruition took about 20 years. It includes wildlife habitats designed to replace those lost from the banks of the Thames because of urban expansion. During its construction, 38 hectares (94 acres) of reed beds and 5 hectares (12 acres) of wet woodland were laid down. A total of 250,000 trees were planted. A wide variety of bird life can be seen, including green woodpeckers, cormorants, lapwings and red kites. The riverbank is well used for recreation by walkers, runners and cyclists. The choice of a name for the river was put to the local population in a poll. The result was a strong preference for 'Jubilee', as it was completed in 2002, the Golden Jubilee of Queen Elizabeth II, whose former main residence, Windsor Castle, is in one of the towns protected by the scheme.

Slough has not generally had a good press since John Betjeman wrote his 1937 poem *Slough*, in which he laments the loss of greenery and the sound of birdsong in the town. While the town was indeed becoming increasingly urbanised and industrialised at that time, this walk shows that the green spaces and the birdsong are still there, less than a mile from Slough railway station in Herschel Park and along the Jubilee River.

Herschel Park, 1 km south of Slough station, is a Grade II-listed park, developed in the mid-19th century as part of a prestigious area of villas. The park has been restored to its Victorian glory with the support of lottery grants and volunteers. The beautiful and valuable historic setting offers a range of recreational, cultural and educational activities, with two small lakes, ancient trees and a nature reserve. Slough Council bought the park and opened it to the public in 1949, renaming it Herschel Park after the astronomer Sir William Herschel, who lived nearby.

Bridge over the River Kennet

18 Reading Circular via the River Kennet, Old Coley Branch Line and Holy Brook

Distance	11 km (7 miles)
Underfoot	Towpaths; tracks; country paths
Start	Reading Station (Elizabeth line; mainline)
Finish	Reading Station
Points of Interest	River Kennet and Kennet Navigation; Fobney Island Nature Reserve; Old Coley Branch Line; Holy Brook
Refreshments	Many opportunities in Reading
Toilets	Reading Station
Shortening the Walk	Leave the walk where it turns onto the old railway. Go up the slope, turn right onto Southcote Farm Lane. After 300m reach Southcote Lane and the No. 26 bus stop.

This is a fascinating excursion with both riverside and countryside on offer, with several distinctly different sections. Reading is the western terminus of the Elizabeth line. After leaving the station, you walk through the town centre, past the Minster Church. However, you soon leave the town behind after joining the River Kennet for an attractive 4 km of towpath, walking past a Nature Reserve and two locks. The Kennet is both a river and a canal (the Kennet Navigation), with navigable stretches of the river connected by canal from the Thames at Reading to Newbury. At Newbury it becomes the Kennet and Avon canal, which goes all the way to Bristol. You leave the river at Southcote Lock and return to Reading firstly via a disused railway line and then on a path along the Holy Brook. You return to the Kennet for a short final stretch back to the town.

Southcote Lock

1. Leave the station and go straight ahead to the town centre, entering the pedestrian zone after traffic lights. Continue to a T-junction by John Lewis and turn right into Broad Street. After 50m, take the first left into a narrow alley, Chain Street. When you reach the church, go diagonally through the churchyard on a brick path. Cross at the traffic lights and go ahead down Bridge Street, towards the large road bridge across the River Kennet. Cross to the right-hand footway at a traffic island.

2. Just before the bridge, take the pedestrian ramp that goes down to the river, which you follow for 3 km, initially on a surfaced path, later on earth and gravel. After going under the A33 road bridge, you walk beside a high industrial fence to the right. At the end of the fence, the path goes left to cross the river at the point where it divides into two, with the River Kennet to the left and the Kennet Navigation and Fobney Lock to the right. Between them is the Fobney Island Nature Reserve. You can choose to walk through the reserve on a firm path, parallel to the towpath, which you rejoin after 500m. Otherwise turn right on the towpath with the canal on your right.

3. After 800m, the canalised section ends and the path goes left to take you back over the river, where you turn right, with the river on your right. 500m later, follow cyclepath signs to the right and go over a small white bridge, where river and canal divide once more. Turn left and then go right on a higher, narrower bridge over the canal, with good views of Southcote Lock. Turn right away from the lock, on a track that swings left to cross a millstream. Continue ahead, following a yellow arrow waymark. After 300m go under a railway bridge and turn right along the railway embankment. When you come to a T-junction, go right under the railway line and then immediately turn left on a paved path

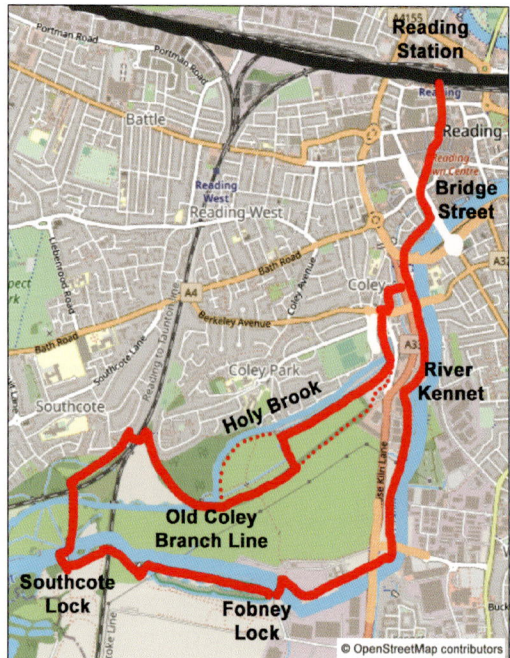

that rises to the level of the track. The path turns away from the railway and goes up a short slope between metal railings. Halfway up, by a cycle and footpath sign, go through a gap in the railings on your right. (*To finish the walk here, continue up the slope to reach a bus route. See details on p.73.*)

4. Descend to the Old Coley Branch Line. Go ahead and follow this level path along the old railway line, soon realising that you are up on a high embankment. After about 450m you can see the Holy Brook down to the right. Shortly after, you cross a bridge over the brook. You now have a choice of three routes.

Option A: The easiest but less scenic route is to simply continue along the old railway line for 1.5 km to a retail park. Go through the car park and walk past the retail units. Turn left into the overflow car park and walk to the far right corner. *Now go to section 5.*

Option B: For the most scenic route, take the steep path down to the left at the end of the bridge to reach the brook. The first few metres might be a bit challenging and you need to be sure of foot. The reward is that after going ahead through a metal gate, you

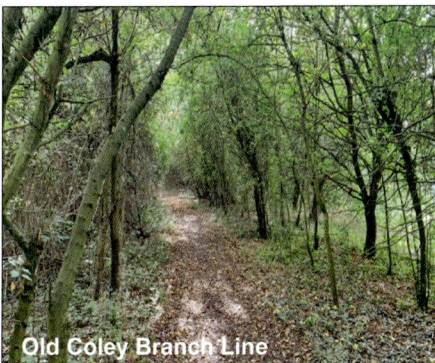
Old Coley Branch Line

reach a lovely stretch along the Holy Brook, which you follow all the way to the outskirts of Reading.

Option C: Continue ahead on the old railway line for another 630m. When you see a small crossing path next to a hump in the path, ignore the path to the right that leads into a field with a pylon visible beyond. Instead, go left through a dilapidated metal farm gate and walk ahead across grass towards a line of houses. After 200m turn right along the bank of the Holy Brook.

Options B and C: Continue along the brook till you reach a high metal fence to the right, after which you enter the overflow car park of a retail centre. (*Please note that some stretches along the Holy Brook can be muddy after rain and overgrown in summer.*)

5. From the overflow car park, look out for a small pedestrian bridge over the Holy Brook. Cross over, then turn left and then right into a road through a small housing estate. At the end, turn left to walk up to a junction with the A4. Cross to the far side of the A4 at the zebra crossing and pedestrian lights. Turn right along the footway. After 15m, go down to the left into St Paul's Court, a private housing estate. Go past the first block and turn right on a permissive path to rejoin the Holy Brook after 50m. Turn left beside the water. After 130m, turn right over a pedestrian bridge and go left on a crossing path. Turn right by a blue cyclepath sign for *Town Centre*. Pass under two road bridges in quick succession. Turn left after the second one and return to the Kennet. Turn left along the river for 350m to reach the bridge where you first joined it. Retrace your steps to Reading Station.

Maidenhead Bridge

19 Taplow Circular via the Jubilee River and the Thames Path

Distance	**11.5 km (7 miles)**
Underfoot	**Mostly riverside paths and tracks; some road walking**
Start	**Taplow Station (Elizabeth line)**
Finish	**Taplow Station**
Points of Interest	**Jubilee River; Dorney Lake; Thames Path; Taplow Village**
Refreshments	**Oak & Saw pub in Taplow Village**
Toilets	**At Taplow Station**
Shortening the Walk	**Return directly from Maidenhead Bridge to Taplow Station via the A4 Bath Road**

Taplow is a small village on the east side of the Thames near Maidenhead. Its name is Anglo-Saxon in origin, and means Tæppa's barrow. The burial mound can still be visited, and important artefacts excavated are on display in the British Museum. The walk starts by crossing the Bath Road and following Marsh Lane south from Taplow Station to reach the Jubilee River, a flood relief channel taking excess water from the Thames above Maidenhead and returning it below Eton. (For a fuller description see page 72.) The walk follows the river for a short distance and then goes cross-country past Dorney Lake to reach the River Thames. The next section is a delightful 4 km walk along the Thames Path past Bray Lock to reach Maidenhead Bridge. The route continues to Taplow village, with its traditional village green, school and local pub, before returning to Taplow Station.

1. From Taplow Station take the Bath Road exit and turn left through the car park. At the end of the access road turn right to reach the A4, Bath Road. Cross carefully at the traffic island as there is no pedestrian phase at the lights. Continue ahead into Marsh Lane. Follow the lane for 1.1 km until you reach a bridge over the Jubilee River by Marsh Lane weir. Cross over the bridge, then turn left on a track sign-posted for *Cycleway 61*, with the river on your left. After 800m, ignore a pedestrian bridge over the river and continue ahead on the right-hand bank towards the M4. Go under the motorway bridge and continue along the river for 500m until you reach a

wooden gate (usually open). After the gate, at a junction of paths, turn right, away from the river, on a path between a fence and a hedge. (The cycleway and footpath signs are not visible until after you have turned right.) Follow the path up to a road with a row of houses on the opposite side. Despite the sign for *Richmond Path*, you are back on Marsh Lane.

2. Turn left and continue for 500m along the footway. Where the road turns left, just past two bungalows, you reach a *Welcome to Eton College & Dorney Lake* sign next to a broad driveway. Turn right here on a signed public footpath to the left of the driveway. Just before you reach a checkpoint by a large metal gate, turn right on a cycle path, signed *Cycleway 4*. Follow the cycle path for 700m along the perimeter fence of the grounds of Eton College, catching glimpses of Dorney Lake to your left through the railings and the trees. Finally, you reach the River Thames and turn right on the Thames Path.

3. Soon the cycleway goes up a ramp to leave the river, but you continue ahead for 4 km along this delightful section of the Thames Path, passing Bray Lock and large riverside mansions. When you reach the outskirts of Maidenhead, you pass under a red-brick railway bridge designed by Brunel. Soon after, you reach the road bridge that takes the Bath Road (A4) over the Thames. The road opposite is Mill Lane. At this point, you

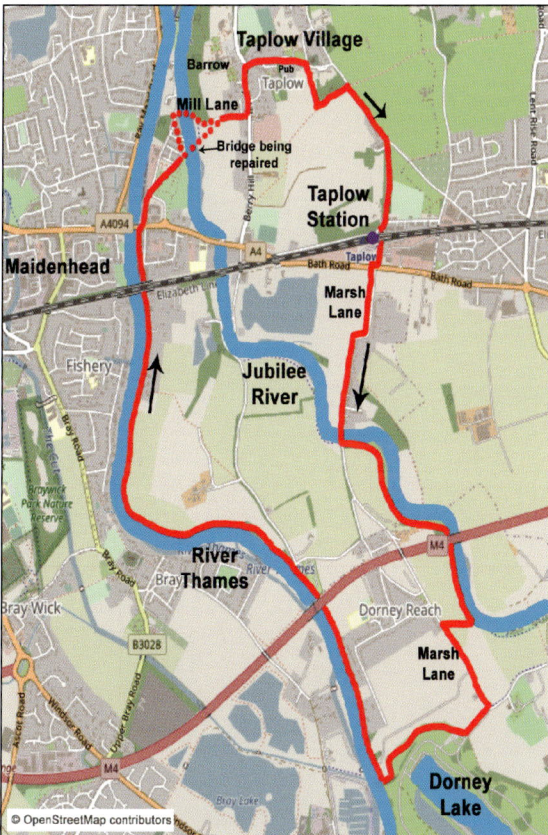

Jubilee River

have walked 8km and you now have two options for completing the walk.

Shorter Option (1.3 km) To go directly back to Taplow Station, turn right on the Bath Road and walk along the footway. After 800m, turn left on the Approach Road to Taplow Station.

4. Longer Option (main walk) (3.5 km) To visit Taplow, cross the Bath Road at the pedestrian lights to your right. Enter Mill Lane and walk through a Berkeley Homes development until you reach Jubilee Lane. Cross over and continue in the same direction on a footpath signed *Taplow Village*, which goes diagonally across a well-maintained park. Follow this path, which leads up to the Jubilee River. At the time of writing, in 2022, the pedestrian bridge ahead over the river had been demolished because it was unsafe. Until the bridge has been replaced, you will need to turn left on a short tarmac path that goes up to a quiet road through a modern development of housing. Go ahead here, with the Jubilee Mill soon visible ahead. When you reach the mill, turn right on Mill Lane following the sign for *Taplow Village*. Cross the river and continue uphill on the lane, ignoring footpaths to left and right, till you reach the T-junction with Berry Hill. Once the bridge has been rebuilt, it will be possible to cut off the corner through the housing development and past the Jubilee Mill by crossing the river on the footbridge and continuing uphill to reach Mill Lane at a higher point, near its junction with Berry Hill.

5. Turn left on Berry Hill and go uphill for about 250m. Cross to the footway

River Thames near Bray Lock

on the right-hand side of the road. Turn right into Rectory Road and continue until you reach the village green, with the Oak and Saw public house on the right. (*If you are thinking about stopping for refreshments, it is worth noting that you still have a good 20-25 minute walk to reach Taplow Station.*) Just after the pub and opposite the church, turn right onto a narrow footpath at the corner of St Nicholas House, by a phone box and a footpath sign. You soon pass the community-run Old Priory Garden on your left (snowdrops in late winter). Go ahead through a metal kissing gate to meet a crossing path and turn left through a wooden gate. Follow this path down to a road (Boundary Road). Turn right and after 900m turn right again into Station Road, which leads to the station.

Footpath to Marsh Lane

Eton Dorney (known as Dorney Lake for the 2012 Olympics) hosted over 400,000 visitors over the games period. Declared the best ever Olympic rowing venue, thirty events were held here. The British team won a total of 12 medals: 6 gold, 2 silver and 4 bronze, making Dorney one of the most successful venues for Team GB.

The Thames Path National Trail, indicated by acorn waymarks, follows the Thames from its source to its official end at the Thames Barrier in Woolwich. It is 296 km (184 miles) long. There is also an extension of the trail to the marshes near Erith. Because the Thames Path is mainly flat, with well-maintained towpaths, many parts of it can be accessed by wheelchair users and walkers of all abilities.

Maidenhead Railway Bridge carries mainline and Elizabeth line trains over the River Thames. It is a single structure of two wide red-brick arches, buttressed by a smaller arch on each river bank. It was designed by Isambard Kingdom Brunel and was completed in 1838. While it was being constructed, the innovative low-rise arches attracted considerable criticism due to their perceived lack of stability. However, to this day, the arches of the structure remain in place and are the flattest to have ever been constructed. The bridge features in a painting by Turner, which is now in the National Gallery. The Thames Path passes under the right-hand arch (facing upstream), which is known as the *Sounding Arch* because of its echo.

Thorndon Country Park

20 Shenfield to Brentwood via Ingrave and Thorndon Country Park

Distance	12 km (7.5 miles)
Underfoot	Paths through woods and fields (muddy stretches in winter and after rain); road walking at start and finish
Start	Shenfield Station (Elizabeth line; mainline)
Finish	Brentwood Station (Elizabeth line)
Points of Interest	Thorndon Hall; Thorndon Country Park
Refreshments	Café in Thorndon Country Park
Toilets	Shenfield and Brentwood Stations; Thorndon Country Pk
Shortening the Walk	Shorter route from Shenfield to Ingrave via Middle Road. See description on p.82. Total distance 9.5 km (6 miles)

This walk explores the countryside to the east and south of Shenfield. The route leading to Ingrave offers wide horizons and passes through a landscape of arable fields and small pockets of woodland. After Ingrave, the walk goes mainly through woods. The highlight of the walk is Thorndon Country Park which has 230 hectares of ancient forests, parkland and ponds, as well as a former deer park, which is now being returned to heathland for grazing. There are many walking trails and some wonderful old trees, including hornbeam and giant oak. The park attracts a large variety of woodland birds, including many migratory birds passing through or spending the winter here. In the summer months, there are many butterflies to be enjoyed. There is also a café and visitor centre. After the country park you walk through Little Warley Common, another area of woodland, which leads all the way to the residential streets of Brentwood.

1. Turn right out of the station and go under the railway bridge. **(For the shorter route turn to p.82.)** Turn into the first road on the right, Mount Avenue, a pleasant tree-lined road through the attractive Hutton Mount Estate. Walk slightly uphill for 700m. When Mount Avenue starts to bear left, turn right into Hillwood Grove. Where the road does a 90-degree turn, take a footpath on the left between hedges. Follow it out to a road and turn left. Turn right at the next junction and then left into Ridgeway. Cross over a main road and arrive at the entrance of St Martin's School. Turn left past a bus stop, and then right onto a signed footpath.

2. The path follows the perimeter of the school grounds. At the end, go past a wooden post with yellow arrows and continue ahead into open countryside across a large arable field. At the far side of the field, turn right on a tarmac farm road. Follow this road and just after it has turned sharp left, go right on a wide gravel bridleway with a faded signpost to *Ingrave Hall*. When you reach a single metal pole across the track, ignore the bridleway sign to the left and go ahead past the pole. Follow the track as it swings right beside some woodland and continue around the perimeter of the field until you come to a large green gate. Go straight ahead past the gate to a T-junction 65m ahead. Turn left on a track towards a house and then right at a footpath sign into a large field with trees on your right. Walk along the perimeter of the field. At a ditch and a hedge, go past the hedge through a gap. Turn left along the other side of the hedgerow, with a field on your right. At the first corner go straight on over a bridge into a small coppice. Turn right to walk down the middle of this pleasant coppice on a permissive path. As you emerge from the trees, join a footpath going in the same direction, with a field

on your left and a hedge and a ditch on your right. Follow the wide grass field margin as the path swings left and then left again by a small wood. 150m after this, watch out for a gap in the hedge, with a plank bridge beyond (the marker post had fallen down in 2022). Go right over the bridge, and follow the green waymark. Walk to the end of the path and turn right on a tarmac path, which brings you out into Middle Road. Go left here and walk up to the main road.

Shorter Route from Shenfield to Ingrave: Turn right out of Shenfield Station and go under the railway bridge. Take the first right into Mount Avenue and then first right again into Herington Grove. After the road curves left, take the first right into Roundwood Avenue. After passing a church, take the second right, Heron Way. Follow this all the way to the end, crossing Ridgeway and going past a 'no through road' sign. Take the footpath straight ahead at the end. You come out into a road by a bus stop and a local shop. Turn left and take the second road on the right, Brindles Close. Immediately turn right on a narrow path. At the end, cross a small wooden bridge. Go ahead on a grass path towards a gap in the hedge, with the view opening up before you. Continue over a field, bearing very slightly left towards a footbridge and a yellow arrow in the hedge opposite. Cross the next small field and go through a hedge onto Middle Road, by houses. Go ahead in the same direction on this quiet lane, with the houses to the left, for 700m to reach Ingrave, where the longer route joins up with Middle Road at Grange Close. Continue to the main road and join the longer route at section 3.

3. Cross at the zebra crossing and turn left. Take the first right into Thorndon Gate by a sign for *Thorndon Park Golf Club*. When you reach a fork with the golf club to the left and Thorndon Hall to the right, your path is straight ahead between the two, signed *Footpath 42*. You follow this shady path past the impressive Thorndon Hall on your right, a former stately home now converted into private residences. Some 80m after the point where the boundary fence goes off to the right, you turn left at a junction by a public footpath sign with its back to you! Continue through the woods with the golf course over to your left. At the end of the path, turn right at a T-junction on a wide track. A few steps further on you pass a sign for *Thorndon Country Park* and reach a broad track that divides into two to your left. Ignore these tracks and cross straight over, entering a former deer enclosure through a gate.

4. Keep right through this area, which is being converted to woodland pasture. Enter a car park through a metal gate and walk up the left-hand side of the car park to reach two gates. Take the gate to the right, following the tea cup sign, which leads onto a gravel path with a green welcome sign. Continue ahead, go down a dip, through a gate and straight over a small crossing path. At

The route near Ingrave

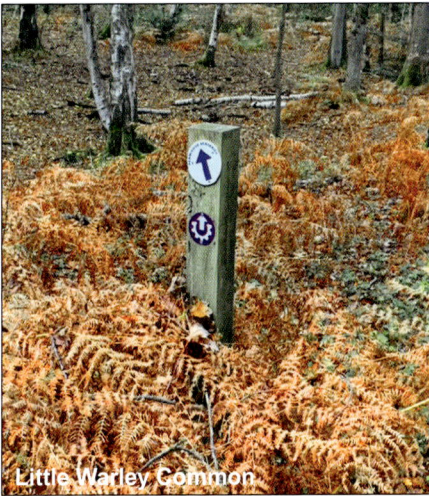

Little Warley Common

the next crossing path, there are public toilets, a café, gift shop and a car park to your right and a picnic area to your left. Continue ahead and go straight over another crossing path. 150m later, turn right at the next crossing path towards some wooden buildings. Just before you reach them, take a narrow path going diagonally left which then swings right and leads to an access road, with two white gatehouses to your right. Turn left here and walk towards a main road. Just before reaching the road, take the firm gravel path to your left which runs parallel to the road, indicated by a *Little Warley Common* board and a wooden sign stating *Hartswood horses and cycles*. After 90m, you reach a wooden post indicating *Hartswood* to the right. Follow this sign, which leads up to the road.

5. Cross with care and enter Little Warley Common Wood by a welcome sign. Route finding may be a little tricky over the next section. Continue ahead, ignoring a path to the left. At a four-way junction, follow the blue arrow sign to

the left, which indicates a permissive horseride. At a fairly indistinct and unmarked fork keep left. At the next fork, bear right towards a blue arrow on a post and swing to the left, following the arrow, ignoring a fork to the right. Watch out for more blue arrows (one of which is hidden in a hollow past a narrow gap between two holly bushes). Cross a wooden bridge and go left, ignoring the bridleway sign to the right and the path straight ahead. There are no waymark arrows on the next stretch but you are walking generally parallel to the road over to your left. At a crossing track, keep straight on. You come up very close to the road, but bear right here to continue through the wood. After 100m emerge on a tarmac road.

6. Turn right, away from a metal gate visible to your left. Walk for 60m and turn left by a white-topped post. Follow this path, passing another white marker post and keeping left in a clearing where a path comes in from the right. Cross a small wooden bridge and follow the yellow arrow to the left. At the next waymark, cross a small stream (which may be dry in summer) and swing to the left following another arrow. At a three-pronged fork stay on the middle path. Go straight over a crossing path, past another yellow arrow. Turn left at the next four-way crossing, towards the road and houses, emerging from the woods opposite South Drive. Cross to the other side, turn right and take the second left, Mount Crescent. Walk the length of this road to a T-junction and turn right into Headley Chase. Take the second right into Warley Mount and walk downhill. It becomes Myrtle Road and goes left above Brentwood Station. Walk to the end and turn right over the bridge to reach the station.

Pages Wood

21 Harold Wood to Rainham along the River Ingrebourne

Distance	**14 km (9 miles)**
Underfoot	**Tarmac tracks and cycle paths; some country footpaths, may be muddy after rain**
Start	**Harold Wood Station (Elizabeth line)**
Finish	**Rainham Station (mainline)**
Points of Interest	**Pages Wood; Upminster Windmill; Ingrebourne Marshes; Ingrebourne Hill**
Refreshments	**Café and pub at Upminster Bridge; pub at Rainham**
Toilets	**Harold Wood Station; Ingrebourne Valley Visitor Centre**
Shorter Option	**Finish at Upminster Bridge Station 7 km (4 miles)**

This is a beautiful walk that explores the southeastern fringes of Greater London by following the course of the River Ingrebourne. You start through Harold Wood Park and enter Pages Wood, a community woodland where 100,000 trees were planted in 2001. You will pass several works of art created by chainsaw sculptor Simon O'Rourke. Next there is 1 km of road walking that takes you safely over the A127 before returning you to the fields beside the river. At Upminster Bridge there is an opportunity for refreshments near the District Line Underground station and a chance to visit a windmill. The second half of the walk follows the lovely Ingrebourne Valley with its wetlands, frequented by many water birds. There is also a visitor centre with toilets and refreshments. You leave the Ingrebourne close to the town of Rainham, which has a mainline train service to Central London.

1. Leave Harold Wood Station via the steps leading up to the Gubbins Lane exit. Turn left across the railway bridge and take the first left into Oak Road, following the green sign for the *London Loop*, which you follow for most of this walk. Take the third road on the right, Archibald Road, which is unmade. The River Ingrebourne is on your left just out of sight, flowing through fields. Walk to the junction with Squirrels Heath Road and turn right. Cross over and take the first left into Brinsmead Road, which leads to Harold Wood Park. Enter the park, turn right and then turn left on a tarmac path just before the car park. Turn left at a T-junction of paths. Cross a bridge over the River Ingrebourne. *(If this bridge is closed, then take another bridge 100m to the left.)*

2. Once on the other side of the river, turn right and follow the path along the side of the river (still mostly hidden from view) passing a *Welcome to Pages Wood* sign. Ignore all paths to the left. The riverside path winds along, following a wooden sculpture trail, created by Simon O'Rourke, depicting wetland wildlife, each with a short poem. After the final sculpture (on a bench) reach a T-junction of paths near an electricity pylon. Turn left here, then take the first right to

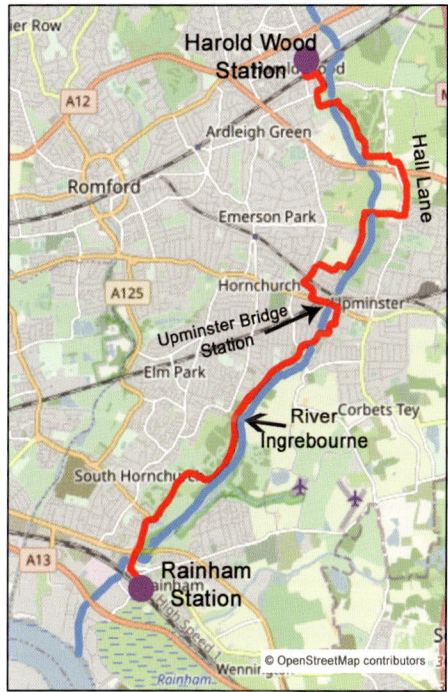

Pages Wood Sculpture Trail

cross a small bridge, with the pylon to the right. Follow the track ahead of you, which climbs a hill. Bear slightly to the right at a 4-way crossing to reach a car park. Go right, following the signs for *Cycleway 136*. Cross Hall Lane, then turn right to walk along the opposite footpath. At a junction, bear left on the cycle path and cross above the A127. Continue on the footway for another 300m, with good views to your right of Canary Wharf, the Shard and the City of London on the skyline. Just after a bus stop, turn left onto a residential side road (Hall Lane), which runs parallel to the main road behind a high hedge.

3. When you reach Avon Road, cross over and turn right to cross the main road at the traffic islands. Go ahead to descend a no-through road, River Drive. Pass through a wooden barrier and enter some thick woodland on Footpath 273. Go ahead with great care on a rough and muddy path. Cross a concrete bridge over the River Ingrebourne, negotiate a broken gate and then cross a small wooden bridge. Turn left, initially along the edge of a large field. Continue ahead as the field opens out to go through a gate and over a small bridge. Ignore a narrow path going straight ahead. Instead take the other narrow path to the left into the woods which leads first down to the river, then meanders between the trees before emerging into a field shortly after a *London Loop* sign.

4. Walk along the left-hand perimeter of the field and continue ahead into a second field. When you reach the opposite side, turn right alongside a hedge. At the next corner cross over a footbridge and turn left towards some houses. When you reach the houses, turn right and walk along the edge of the field. Just before the next corner, leave the field to the left on a narrow footpath leading to a road. Swing right then left to join Wingletye Lane and continue in the same direction to cross over a hump-backed railway bridge. Turn left into Minster Way. Walk to the end to the junction with

the Upminster Road (the A124). To your left is Upminster Bridge Station. You have now walked 6.5 km (4 miles) since leaving Harold Wood. If you feel in need of refreshments there is a café across the road on the right.

5. To continue to Rainham, turn left and walk past Upminster Bridge tube station and the Windmill pub. The sails of the windmill are just visible above the rooftops. Take the third road on the right, Bridge Avenue. (*To visit the windmill, go ahead for 350m then return to this point.*) There is no street name visible but there are signs for the *London Loop* and *Hornchurch Sports Stadium* on the left-hand side of the A124 pointing the way. Walk along Bridge Avenue for 400m, then turn right between some hedges towards Hornchurch Football Stadium (*London Loop sign obscured by a hedge*). Turn left before reaching the stadium gates into a car park. Keep left to climb a small ramp. You are now on a path that leads all the way to Rainham.

6. Cross over a bridge and turn immediately left. After 100m the path turns briefly away from the river to cross a road at traffic lights. It then

Ingrebourne Marshes

returns to the river bank. You pass a sign for the *Ingrebourne Valley*. Go ahead, ignoring all turnings to the left or right, to reach a play area and a visitor centre, with a café, toilets and a gift shop. Carry on until you reach a signpost with a choice of routes to a lake. Take the left-hand path. You come to a viewing area over the marshes with an information panel. Continue on the path, bearing right at the signpost to *Albyns Farm*. Go ahead to reach a lake on your right. At the end of the lake, turn right on the tarmac path and walk for 200m to reach a walled house (Albyns Farm) on your right. Shortly afterwards, turn left on a track. When the track ends, go right between wooden posts and

then turn left to continue in the same direction as before. After 350m, at the top of a short incline, there is a path to the left to the top of Ingrebourne Hill. Take the winding path up to the summit and continue downhill on the other side, past a lake, to reach a car park. Pass to the right of the car park and walk out to a busy road. Turn left and after 300m reach The Albion pub. Continue to a roundabout and use the pedestrian lights to continue ahead. Cross the Ingrebourne for the last time over Red Bridge. Go across the access road of a large supermarket and turn left on Bridge Road. Follow it past the 12th century parish church. You soon reach Old Station Lane and turn right to Rainham Station.

Harold Wood is a suburban neighbourhood of Romford in the London Borough of Havering. It is situated 26.6 km (16.5 miles) east of central London near the Greater London boundary with Essex. The name Harold Wood was first recorded in 1237.

Pages Wood Sculpture Trail is part of the Land of the Fanns project in cooperation with Forestry England. This series of wooden sculptures along the Ingrebourne was created by Simon O'Rourke, known for his work on *Game of Thrones*. The trail depicts Verity Vole, who introduces each wildlife creature with a charming short poem.

Upminster Windmill was built in 1803 and was once known as Abraham's Mill. It is 16m high and has a boat-shaped cap with a gallery. Four sails are carried on a cast-iron windshaft. In 2004 the Upminster Windmill Preservation Trust was granted a 35-year lease on the mill. At the time of writing, in 2022, it was still being restored to working order, but visits should be possible once this has been completed.

The River Ingrebourne rises near Brentwood and flows for 43 km (27 miles) in a south-westerly direction to enter the Thames at Rainham. Ingrebourne Marshes are a Site of Special Scientific Interest due to the diversity of birds and other wildlife in the beds of wetland reeds.

Rainham lies on the outskirts of East London and is historically part of the county of Essex. It is located in an area that is highly susceptible to flooding. The nearby marshlands beside the River Thames are only 1.5m above sea level.

The London Loop is a 242 km-long waymarked path around the outer edges of London, making good use of public footpaths though woods, parks, fields, pastures and along rivers. It is divided into 24 stages that can be easily walked in a day. *Loop* describes not only the shape of the walk but stands for London Outer Orbital Path.

Raphael Park

22 Romford to Harold Wood via four Public Parks and Havering-atte-Bower

Distance	14.5 km (9 miles)
Underfoot	Paved surfaces; tarmac paths; country paths, some muddy stretches in winter or after rain
Start	Romford Station (Elizabeth line; mainline)
Finish	Harold Wood (Elizabeth line)
Points of Interest	Lodge Farm Park; Raphael Park; Rise Park; Bedfords Park; Havering-atte-Bower Village and Water Tower
Refreshments	Cafés in Romford and near Harold Wood Station. Visitor Centre in Bedfords Park (*check website for opening times*)
Toilets	Romford Station; Harold Wood Station
Shorter Option	Finish at Havering-atte-Bower, 7.5km (5 miles)

Romford is a historic market town with a busy town centre. This is an interesting walk through some lovely countryside. It traces a route through a series of four parks stretching north from the centre of Romford. Lodge Farm Park is followed by a waterside stretch through Raphael Park and Rise Park leads on to the open expanses of Bedfords Country Park. Apart from a section of road-walking to cross the busy A12, most of the walk is very green. The halfway point is the pretty village of Havering-atte-Bower, which has an infrequent bus service back to Romford Station from Monday to Saturday. Check bus times before you go if you wish to shorten the walk. The second half follows the London Loop footpath through remote open countryside. The final section is on a ribbon of parkland which leads down to Harold Wood.

1. Turn left out of Romford Station and take the second right into Western Road. After 300m you come to a large roundabout. Cross at the pedestrian lights on your right to continue along Western Road to its end. Turn left and take the first right into Sims Close. At the end by the turning circle, continue ahead to Lodge Farm Park. Turn left and walk through the park, passing a miniature railway, complete with its own station. Shortly after the tennis courts, cross the road at the lights to enter Raphael Park. Take the path to the left and go along the water's edge to the end of the lake. Follow the path as it turns right and then turn left onto an unsurfaced path between trees. Where the path turns right, go left over a small bridge to leave the park. Your onward route now follows some residential streets to reach the safe crossing over the A12. Go up Parkland Avenue and turn right on Pettits Lane. Cross to the left-hand pavement and walk towards the traffic sign for the A12, visible ahead. Cross via the footbridge and continue in the same direction. Turn right into Beauly Way by the Fire Station. Go past Clyde Way and Dee Way and turn left into Rise Park. Follow the path signed *Thomas England Walk* along the left-hand perimeter of the park. Continue past a lightly wooded stretch to reach Lower Bedfords Road. Cross at the lights and enter Bedfords Country Park.

2. Ignore the path ahead to the top of a small hill. Instead go diagonally right towards a kissing gate. Go through the gate, across a plank bridge and up a short slope. Turn left and go up through a gate set back in a hedge into the next field. Your route goes diagonally right towards two metal gates on the opposite side. At a grassy fork, aim for the gate on the left. Go through the kissing gate and follow a gravel track as it swings left up a hill. Ignore any paths to right and left. By a bench near the top, take a look back to admire the view. Continue ahead on a wide path through trees. Reach an open grassy area where the land drops away to your left. Walk towards a car park in the distance ahead. Just after entering the car park, take the path to the right to the Visitor Centre (*café, gift shop, toilets*) with picnic tables and views of the deer park and the countryside beyond.

3. Facing the Visitor Centre, take the tarmac path to the left and then go left on a wider track that takes you back to the top end of the car park. Go across the car park entrance to the left of a yellow arrow and walk along a grassy path through woodland, parallel to the park access road over to your right. The path finally leads to an open grassy area. Continue ahead towards a small car park. Go to the left of the car park and cross another open green space, still following the line of the road off to your right. Soon you see a white tower ahead. This is the Havering-atte-Bower water tower, built by the South Essex Waterworks Company in 1934 in the style of a Norman tower. Walk towards it and exit the park between two wooden markers behind a bench. Turn left on a tarmac footway which soon joins the road. Continue with wide views towards Romford on your left. When you reach the junction with North Road, turn right to reach Havering-

Havering-atte-Bower Water Tower

atte-Bower. Pass a bus stop on the right-hand side of the road for buses back to Romford Station. (*The 357 bus route is very infrequent and only runs Monday to Saturday. If you plan to finish here, do check the bus timetable before setting out.*)

4. 150m after the bus stop, pass a sign for resident parking. Turn right here by a sign *Footpath No 7 Paternoster Row*, with a *London Loop* sign below. Go through a tight entrance between a garage and a bush onto a narrow path towards a small gate which leads into open fields. Go ahead with an electric fence and fields to your left and a ditch to your right. You soon see the water tower you passed earlier. When you are on a level with the tower, turn left at a junction by a metal gate, pass another gate and a *London Loop* sign and go down the side of the field with trees on your right. After 200m turn right over a footbridge with a kissing gate at either end. Go past a footpath post and continue over the brow of the next field and slightly to the right to a gate in the opposite side. Go through to the next field and continue ahead past a lone tree towards a fingerpost with a *London Loop* sign. Turn right along the field, with a wood on your left. Go left at a corner (*London Loop*) and continue to follow the boundary of the wood. To your left you can see a large farmhouse. At the next corner ignore a squeeze stile into a paddock opposite. Instead, go left towards a dilapidated wooden fingerpost next to a small mound covered in nettles. The fingerpost indicates the *London Loop* to the right between the mound and the electric fence of the paddock. This path is not recommended as it is not well-maintained. Instead, go past

Near Havering-atte-Bower

ends at a gate and a stile. Go over the stile into Cummings Hall Lane and turn left, passing a bench before reaching a main road (Noak Hill Road). Turn left by the Deer's Rest pub. (*To finish the walk here, take a 294 bus to Harold Wood Station from the bus stop opposite the pub.*) To continue, go past the pub to a roundabout and turn right into Tees Drive. When you reach Priory Road, ignore a *London Loop* sign to the left, as this section of the path along a brook is blocked by fallen trees. Instead, carry on down Tees Drive to its junction with Whitchurch Road.

the small mound and turn right on a broad grassy farm track. After 300m the track swings left and you follow it towards a wood, where you find another *London Loop* sign. Continue with the wood on your right to a corner and turn left at a waymark.

5. After 320m you reach a footbridge into a field on the right with a *London Loop* marker hidden in the hedge. In 2022 this bridge was not safe to cross. To avoid it, continue for 40m to a gap in the hedge. Go through into a field and turn right and then left along its boundary towards a *London Loop* marker post in the neighbouring field, on the opposite side of a ditch. If the ditch is dry and you feel it is safe, then cross over onto the official path. If not, stay to the left of the ditch until you reach a hedgerow. A short way along the hedge, cross into the other field via a farm track. Back on the official route along the field edge, which is rather narrow here, continue to a stile in the corner of the field. Cross the stile into Paternoster Row. Follow the signs to the right and continue to the end of the lane. Shortly before reaching a gate across the lane, go over a signposted stile to the left and follow this byway until it

6. Cross over and go slightly to the left to enter a tarmac path with the brook now on your right. Follow the path, or simply walk straight across the grass, to another road (Dagnam Park Drive). Cross over and continue into Central Park, initially with a high fence on your right. Stay on this path as it swings first right then left, passing a playground and a refreshment hut. At a 'roundabout' continue ahead on a broad cycle track towards a car park. Go through the car park to Petersfield Avenue. Cross over and continue ahead on a joint cycle and pedestrian path. Cross another road (St Neot's Road) for the last stretch along the brook before the path veers left and then right through a gate to reach the A12. It is unsafe to cross the dual carriageway here, so turn right on the footway and walk towards the traffic lights visible ahead. At the junction, use the pedestrian lights to cross to the left and enter Gubbins Lane for the last 500m to Harold Wood station.

91

River Thames between Cookham and Bourne End

23 Maidenhead to Marlow via Cookham, Bourne End and the Thames Path

Distance	15.5 km (10 miles)
Underfoot	Country and riverside paths; a few muddy stretches in winter or after rain
Start	Maidenhead (Elizabeth line; mainline)
Finish	Mainline from Marlow or Bourne End to Maidenhead
Points of Interest	Ancient waterways; Wood sculptures; Cookham; Marlow
Refreshments	Maidenhead; Cookham; Bourne End; Marlow
Toilets	Maidenhead Station
Shorter Option	Finish at Bourne End Station, 9 km (5.5 miles)

Maidenhead is a market town in Berkshire 43 km (27 miles) west of Central London. Its name derives from Saxon times - *maiden hythe* is thought to mean 'new wharf'. This is a fascinating walk that follows some of the old Maidenhead waterways through the remnants of ancient common land to the north of the town. These channels were once important as a flood defence, but in many cases have now run dry or become overgrown. A local project is underway to restore them for recreational and environmental purposes. Beyond the waterways is the pretty village of Cookham, with a picturesque high street and several pubs and tea shops. The artist Stanley Spencer lived here and his works are exhibited in a former chapel on the High Street. A highlight of the route is the glorious walk along the Thames Path from Cookham to the charming town of Marlow via Bourne End. Along the way you will see many impressive riverside houses, rowers training on the river and red kites flying overhead.

1. From the platform at Maidenhead Station go down the steps to the underpass and take the exit by Platform 1, signed *Taxis* and *Buses*. Turn left and walk to the T-junction with Braywick Road. Cross at the lights and go ahead on a footpath signed *Retail Park* and *Cyclepath 4*. Follow the path as it turns right along the side of a multi-storey car park. Go left at the end, with a retail centre ahead of you. Turn right, walk up to the main road and turn left. Just after a set of pedestrian lights, cross a bridge and turn left beside the York Stream by a sign for *Green Way to Cookham.* Pass the first of several wooden sculptures named the *Guardians of the Green Way*. Wood sculptures and the *Green Way* signs accompany you all the way to Cookham. Go through a pedestrian underpass and cross a small road. Continue ahead to reach the High Street where the York Steam disappears under the Chapel Arches Bridge,

2. Turn right on the High Street, cross over and take the first left into a short road. At the end, turn left in front of Arena Court, on a footway beside railings. You rejoin the York Stream at a small bridge. Do not cross the bridge, but take the steep steps down to the right, with the water on your left. Go under a road bridge, and continue ahead along the river. (*Please note that the footpath under the bridge may*

be waterlogged.) You reach a reed-filled watercourse (the Moor Cut) which may be dry in summer. Turn right to cross a wooden bridge. After the bridge turn left, still following the *Green Way* signs. Continue on this pleasant path with the York Stream on your left, passing some more wooden sculptures. The path crosses to the opposite bank on a wooden bridge just before a road. Cross over and continue ahead on a firm path which twists and turns through a grassy paddock. At a crossing path, continue straight ahead, following *Green Way* and *Cyclepath 50* signs. When you reach a pond on your left, there is an area of open common land (Town Moor) ahead, with houses over to the left. Go ahead on a grass path, initially parallel to a car-wide track. Continue along the right-hand perimeter of the

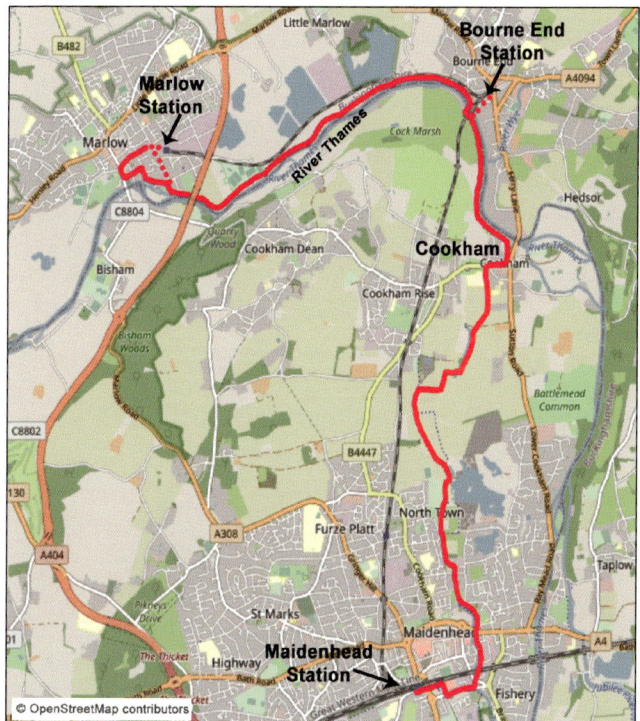

common, with a hedge to your right. At the top right-hand corner, go through a gate to a junction with a small road.

3. Cross the road via a zebra crossing and go ahead between two metal posts to the right of a metal fence. Cross a bridge (the York Stream again), turn left and arrive at a fork. Ignore the broad cycle track which goes straight ahead and take the smaller path going diagonally to the left, signed *Green Way West*. Follow this path for 800m alongside the Maidenhead Ditch, keeping ahead at all junctions, with the water always on your left. Continue past a prominent bank, dotted with trees (by a bridge with signs for *Maidenhead Boundary Walk*). Walk for another 200m to a second bank, with a *Green Way West* sign pointing right. Go right, along the top of the bank, until you reach a hedge and a number of waymarks. Go left here, following a *Green Way West* sign, on a well-defined path through the middle of a cultivated field. At the other side of the field, turn right, following the *Green Way* sign over a small bridge. Do not follow the yellow *Green Way* marker to the left as you step off the bridge. Instead, continue

ahead on a tree-lined path with a small watercourse, the White Brook, on your right. Cross another bridge and go left at a *Green Way East* sign. You stay on Green Way East for the next 1.5 km to Cookham, initially beside another ancient watercourse, the Strand Water. After 600m the path swings away from the Strand and heads across a field towards a distant hedge line. Over to your right in the distance, Cliveden House is just visible high above the Thames. You continue on an enclosed path between fences. Look out here for some intriguing art installations on private land, including a bear on a pole eating ice cream and a little later, set back from the path, an imposing wooden figure of a Native American. You reach Cookham at the access road to Moor Hall Conference Centre. Turn right down the road to reach the war memorial and a bus stop.

4. Turn right here into the High Street, where there is a choice of tea shops and pubs. At the end of the High Street, just after the Stanley Spencer Gallery in a former chapel on your right, turn left and then a few steps further on, go left again into Church Gate, past a small group of attractive

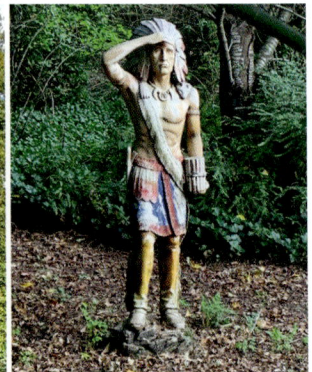

Wooden sculptures along the way

Cookham Church

cottages, towards Holy Trinity Church. Follow the *Thames Path* sign across the churchyard to reach the River Thames. Turn left and follow the riverbank for 1.3 km. This is a really delightful section along the wide-flowing Thames, with many beautiful houses on the opposite bank. You reach a green railway bridge. Ignore a path to the left here and stay close to the river to go under the bridge. Climb the steps to the left and follow the *Thames Path* signs to cross the river via a footbridge to the left of the railway lines.

To finish the walk at Bourne End, turn right and go under the bridge. Almost immediately, turn left through a gap at the end of some railings. Climb the concrete steps and turn right beside the railway track. You soon reach the station, where there are train and bus services back to Maidenhead.

5. To continue to Marlow, turn left as you come down from the bridge and follow the Thames Path all the way to Marlow. Once you have left the houses, marina and sailing clubs of Bourne End behind, you enter a quiet section of open meadows. 4 km after leaving Bourne End railway bridge, you go under a road bridge carrying the A404. The path becomes surfaced and you soon reach the first houses of Marlow. The Thames Path now turns

away from the river, past a metal barrier and reaches Mill Road. At this point you have two options.

To go directly to Marlow Railway Station (14 km total) Turn right on Mill Road, then left into Lock Road. Continue for 600m till you see a sign for the station, opposite the Marlow Donkey pub. Turn right here on Station Approach.

To finish the walk via Marlow Town Centre (15.5 km total) Turn left along Mill Road and follow it as it skirts round the residential complex of Marlow Mill. You pass a sign for Marlow Lock. (*A short detour to the lock takes you to an iconic viewpoint of the weir and Marlow suspension bridge.*) Mill Road swings right and after passing Thamesfield Gardens on your right, you turn left to follow the *Thames Path* sign down an alley between brick walls, known as Seven Corners Alley. Emerge on a road with a slipway to your left and the Two Brewers pub on your right. Turn right, cross over and go left into an alley following a *Thames Path* sign. You come out into the town centre by the church. To your left is the elegant suspension bridge over the Thames. Across the road is Higginson Park with many fine trees, riverside views and a brick and grass maze, which was created to celebrate the Millennium. To your right is the attractive High Street. To reach the station, turn right past the George and Dragon pub into Station Road and walk for 450m to reach a crossroads by the Marlow Donkey pub. Cross over and go down Station Approach to the unmanned station, which has a shuttle service to Maidenhead via Bourne End.

OTHER TITLES FROM COUNTRYSIDE BOOKS

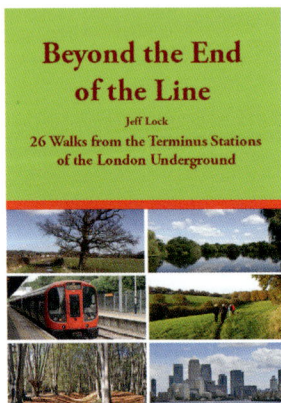

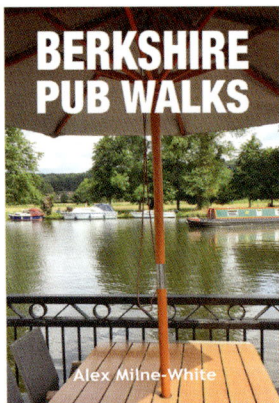

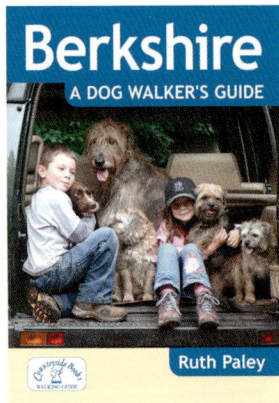

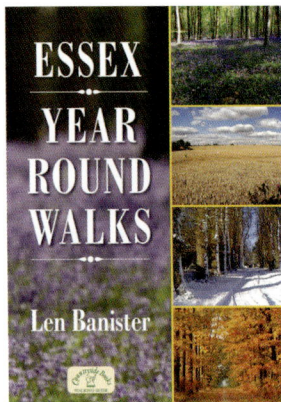

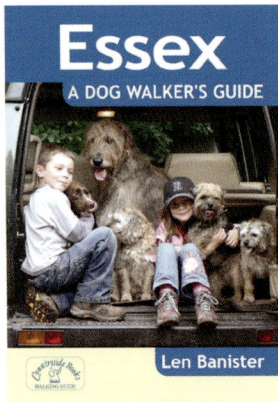

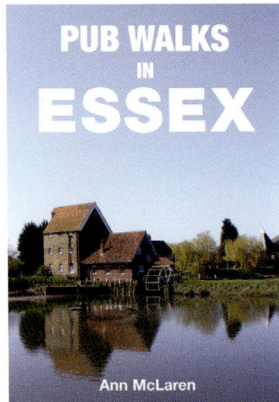

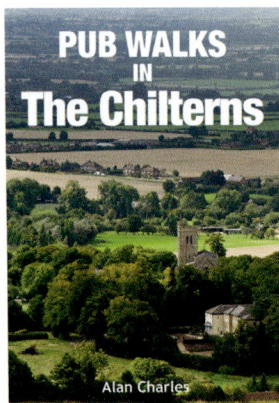

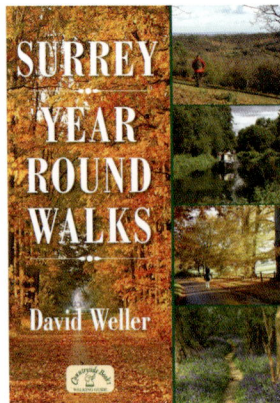

Beyond the End of the Line

Jeff Lock

26 Walks from the Terminus Stations of the London Underground

BERKSHIRE PUB WALKS

Alex Milne-White

Berkshire
A DOG WALKER'S GUIDE

Ruth Paley

ESSEX YEAR ROUND WALKS

Len Banister

Essex
A DOG WALKER'S GUIDE

Len Banister

PUB WALKS IN ESSEX

Ann McLaren

PUB WALKS IN The Chilterns

Alan Charles

KENT DOG FRIENDLY PUB WALKS

DAVID & HILARY STAINES

SURREY YEAR ROUND WALKS

David Weller

To see our full range of books please visit
www.countrysidebooks.co.uk
Follow us on @CountrysideBooks